Also by Saeed Teebi

Her First Palestinian and Other Stories

YOU WILL NOT KILL OUR IMAGINATION

A Memoir of Palestine and Writing in Dark Times

SAEED TEEBI

Published by Scribner Canada

NEW YORK   AMSTERDAM/ANTWERP   LONDON
TORONTO   SYDNEY/MELBOURNE   NEW DELHI

SCRIBNER
C A N A D A

An Imprint of Simon & Schuster, LLC
166 King Street East, Suite 300
Toronto, Ontario M5A 1J3

This Scribner Canada edition September 2025

SCRIBNER CANADA and colophon are trademarks of
Simon & Schuster, LLC

Interior design by Paul Dippolito

Manufactured in the United States of America

3   5   7   9   10   8   6   4   2

Online Computer Library Center number: 1492377779

ISBN 978-1-6680-8466-3
ISBN 978-1-6680-8467-0 (ebook)

For my family

Contents

1 Fear and Bodies 1

2 Reclamation and Rebuilding 39

3 Clarity and Blur 69

4 Stories and Their Telling 103

5 Platform and Safety 139

6 The Company and You 171

7 Imagination 205

Acknowledgements 221

YOU WILL NOT KILL OUR IMAGINATION

– 1 –

Fear and Bodies

A chasm of time ago, in the spring of 2022, I moved to the suburbs. My family was fledgling. After my first marriage ended some years earlier, I began a second one in 2019. Then came a baby girl the following year, at a crest in the pandemic. We had outgrown our rental in the Junction area of Toronto. The sedate rhythms of Oakville suited my wife, a committed suburbanite.

When we took possession, we removed our masks and breathed the quietude. Our new house had an extension that flooded it with light. There was a ravine behind the fence of our backyard. We had a kitchen island that on its own was larger than the whole kitchen of our previous place.

The house also had a staircase, exposed all the way to the top. Dark-varnished treads and handrails, with wrought iron balusters. The staircase rose in a seashell whorl up to a skylight, which cast a gentle illumination down upon it. When you entered the house, you could see all the way up to the second floor. It was easy to think: How many years before my daughter descends this staircase in a wedding dress?

Our early days brought predictable excitements and apprehensions. The revelation that we had gone so long without hearing a fire engine howl. The glee swirled with anxiety about filling all this new space. Decoding which of the neighbours were friendly, and which needed to be treated with delicacy. But a feeling I did not anticipate was that I would be terrified of my own second floor.

The staircase. I kept thinking about that staircase, how high and how exposed it was. How a thing could fall from up there, and how much that thing could suffer in the brief journey. A small, fragile thing could plummet, carom against a hard railing, and hit a tread or two before landing, probably in a form unlike the one it started with.

I kept thinking of my daughter—eighteen months old at the time—wriggling and bucking in my arms as we passed by the staircase from our bedroom to hers, or vice versa. How unsteady my footsteps can feel as I'm carrying her, how clumsy and unsafe are my arms.

At first I dismissed these as just intrusive thoughts. I am mostly immune to irrational agitations of this nature. This is owing less to innate poise than to a kind of lifelong recklessness, and a tendency to forget the hurts I sustain, big or small. I simply do not dwell on things that could injure me or others. When I do, I seem to have a higher tolerance for danger than most.

But the staircase was a different matter. I was obsessed with the thought of my daughter falling from that height. With her fragility, it could be fatal. I obsessed most over how I might be the cause of such a fall, that somehow I would trip while holding her, or that my hands would spontaneously spasm.

The visions—for that's what they became—took on a certain thickness in their character, an omnipresence. No longer were they confined to short, imagistic blurts when I passed by the staircase; they now came to me when I was on my living room sofa, reading or watching TV. They came to me when I was driving to work or taking a walk trying to conjure words for my writing. They were vivid and sustained enough to be viscerally hurtful. Sometimes they were so overpowering I'd let out a small, involuntary scream.

The problem got so severe that I talked to my wife about it, which I did not do lightly. She was already possessed of an extensive catalogue of phobias that I hesitated to add to. But all she did was nod that yes, we do have to be careful around the stairs. There was no terror in her eyes at all.

By now the visions had become laced with impossible elements. My baby daughter would, on the way down, be torn and mutilated in ways that were beyond the capacity of a simple fall. Sometimes there would be flames enveloping her. Sometimes this small person that I adored—sometimes she would be thrown.

The visions were never about hurting myself on the stairs. Only my daughter, over and over.

My new house felt like it had sustained irreparable pollution. The visions were a persistent smear on my surroundings, the new furniture and the new paint. When we were upstairs, I no longer trusted myself to carry my daughter, so I made her walk, even early in the mornings when she still wanted bodily warmth and her little feet were wobbly. As she walked I reminded her in a sharp tone to stay as far away as possible when she passed the railing. If she insisted I carry her, I locked my arms all around her like a football, flexing to an ache, and I moved sideways, crablike, with my back to the staircase. An absurd sight, but I had to minimize the risk.

I've never considered the act of writing to be therapeutic, but I did think of writing a short story about the visions. It would be the grisliest of horror stories, I told my wife, a total departure for me. Perhaps then the visions would let me go. But there is a moment in a narrative when you expect a solution to emerge, or otherwise for the story to reach a horrible climax. I had none of the former and no stomach for the latter.

Eventually I had to come to terms with what my visions

reminded me of: my father and balconies. My father could not bear seeing me or any of my siblings go near one. If we did, he would rush to scold and yank us out of the danger zone, our thin arms smarting from the roughness.

But it did not make sense to me that I'd inherited this fear from my father. From my previous marriage I'd had a son, who was now in his teenage years. I'd never felt these irrational fears for him when he was a child. Why, now, was I possessed by this new impulse to overprotect? I was in my forties. How could an inherited fear spring up so late in life?

I put this question to the contractor I brought in to give me an estimate for walling up the staircase. For a few months before that moment, the visions had ebbed. My daughter was older. She could handle herself, rarely even allowing me to carry her anymore. Sometimes I could even pass by the staircase without a horrible notion invading my psyche. But in late 2023, the visions came back again, torrid with heat. My daughter's body felt so endangered to me.

I didn't know how long I'd have to live like this. I needed a resolution. This was supposed to be a home.

By now, of course, the precariousness of Palestinian bodies has been demonstrated with a brutality and frankness unseen in contemporary history. When I first had my visions, they were, despite their force and immediacy, at a remove. It felt clear to me that they were imaginative visions. This meant I could dismiss them. Once they had passed, I could separate myself from them, rationalizing that they had no connection to reality, not really. My actual eyes, the organs in my skull, had not seen the horrors.

I would have never expected that these eyes would, starting in October 2023, see so many real Palestinian bodies destroyed in so many different ways. Many of the bodies were as small as my daughter's, and smaller. What was I supposed to do with these new, far more horrific sights?

The hoariest of writerly clichés is that the role of the writer is to witness. Whether it originates from a feeling of ineffectuality in the face of intractable problems, or from an earnest faith in witness and documentation, I find its durability surprising. Not long ago I read a new novel by a renowned author that centered on artists living through various European wars; at the end, the curative value of the artist as witness was proffered as some kind of epiphany. But as my smartphone had for months tingled every hour of every day with new footage and documentation of an Israeli killing rampage that showed no signs of abating despite unprecedented levels of witnessing, I wanted to heave the book at a wall.

And yet I couldn't help but keep witnessing. As a Palestinian living in exile, witnessing calamity from afar is an entrenched life feature. Since the turn of the last century Palestinians have been subject to Zionist violence as a matter of course, nearly to the point of inurement. But the war on Gaza was an entirely new outgrowth of that diurnal violence, a thing almost too astonishing for my brain. After alarm and worry and panic and shock and horror and rage and grief had all taken their turns in my emotional system, I noticed that I was gripped longest by a sort of bewilderment at it all. Not just at the volume of killing, but how multifarious it was.

We innately understand that there is a way to kill that, if it does not exactly honour the victim—because murder can never honour anyone—then at least respects their having been a human, their having been a life in the same way as their killer is a life. But the manner in which Israel murdered Palestinians after October 7 was so varied in its cruelty as to feel like an exercise in macabre creativity, like a performance that *wants* a witness. We saw countless bodies, an unending corpse exhibition, to use the phrase of the Iraqi writer Hassan Blasim. Every day when the curtains of our lives drew open, we saw them: soot-gray bodies strewn in the wrecks of their former dwellings, bodies twirling and burning in fire, bodies pockmarked with nodules of gunpowder so numerous they seem like a wallpaper pattern, bodies striped with the serialized cuttings of an inanimate drone, bodies scorched into shades ranging from meat pink to dusk red to crisp black, bodies with blown stumps where their necks once were, bodies with their hearts still beating as they look at their shredded limbs dangling from them like hay from a broomstick, bodies still measured by womb age left to starve and decompose in intensive care incubators, bodies where the final, dark violation is evinced by a bloody circle soaking the fabric covering their genitals, bodies frozen to death in cold tents, bodies squeezed under bulldozer chains into a spongy, fruit-like pulp, small bodies with a solitary round black hole in their foreheads, bodies being gnawed (in real time, as the camera rolls) by famished cats and dogs, bodies lying on the forensicist's table with a notebook next to them detailing markers of sexual defilement, bodies with Down syndrome gored to their screaming death by army canines, bodies blown into parts small enough to fit into cooking pots, then gathered from the streets by relatives to carry in butcher bags, bodies pushed lazily off the rooftops of their houses, bodies vaporized without a trace like they had been not creatures but mere thoughts, bodies in shrouds arranged together on the ground into one last family portrait, nude bodies in lineups walking on their knees to an executioner, bodies whose heads have a soldier's foot resting atop them as the soldier preens for a friendly lens, and bodies that only exist in inference, in the vast rubble, not dignified with even a last pair of eyes to gaze upon them in love or hatred.

It wasn't only the precariousness of the bodies, but

their cheapness. How unproblematic it was to dispatch them, in ever more experimental ways. I thought of dollar store figurines, the mutilation of which perturbs neither the psychotic child nor their parents.

It burned me most that so many of the bodies we saw were young ones. Early in the genocide I wrote for a national paper an article in which I was aghast at how many children had already been killed. The number I quoted at the time was a thousand dead children. Now I think of that figure with a strain of grotesque wistfulness; it has since been multiplied dozens of times over. The youth of the victims sometimes felt incidental to the whole genocidal affair, a signal that Israel's harvesting of humans did not care about metrics of their identity like age; this stood to reason, since the West has always relied on indiscriminateness as a guiding principle of the wars it wages against the Other, from Vietnam to Afghanistan to Iraq. But I am not so naive to believe Israel's crime is mere indiscriminateness. I remember Muhammad al-Durrah, from the year 2000, gunned down even as he crouched under the wing of his father. I remember the Bakr cousins, from the year 2014, all four of them shelled as they were playing soccer on the beach on a day clear with sun.

Filling a soldier's crosshairs with children must be attractive because of how *unfulfilled* children are. They are engines vibrating with energy and imagination, fueled by their families' devotion. They have decades of desire

9

ahead of them, of ambition, of readiness to impose themselves and their will. They have more left of every innate resource than I could ever hope to have at my age, and I will always feel it a strange verdict of fate that I should survive and they don't.

I want to be self-conscious about my witnessing because it helps with the prejudices that I am working against. My own prejudices, before those of others. A few paragraphs back I wrote that by now the precariousness of Palestinian bodies has been demonstrated—that was my diction. It shames me that, as a person who has lived his whole life in a Palestinian body, I have felt that, *finally*, things have now been *demonstrated* beyond argument. That, finally, enough Palestinians have been brutalized. That, finally, we can give a rest to all our illustrative bar graphs and citation-laden reports and meticulous histories, because we have an incontrovertible data point for the vast disproportion of human cost in this supposed "conflict." That, finally, what we always said about the cruelty and unjustness of those who perpetrate this against us has been vindicated.

But the denial of the experience of Palestinians has always been key to rendering their bodies so precarious, so cheap. I've internalized the denial so much that I feel it in my heart whenever I speak about being Palestinian—it is a half-thump, a bracing, a dry throat, a foreknowledge of the coming retort. When I offer a fact or even a piece of personal history, I am already aware that what I said is a claim. It was *not* a fact, or even personal history. It was a claim that, absent proof, exists in the purgatory of the unsubstantiated. It will eventually be refuted by some more legitimate source than me, the body that lived it. At minimum there will be a counterclaim. And in the gap between claim and counterclaim, the truth will fall, limp and untrustworthy.

But I have to resist this feeling. For each of the bodies I witnessed, I suppressed the desire to add a footnote to substantiate it. I will not prove that the bodies existed, that the starving and families existed. I saw them with my eyes. Even if I footnoted every last story of every last Palestinian death with a picture of them bloodied and expired, it wouldn't make a difference. Some will doubt the pictures are real. If the pictures are real, they will doubt the deaths are real. If the deaths are real, they will doubt the stories showing the unjustness of the deaths are real, or that the stories were told fairly.

In a world of polarities, how one conceives of a people's destruction is necessarily an indication of where they lie on some spectrum of thought. The construct of the spectrum abstracts the reality of the genocide and turns identifying it as such into a symptom of our personal bias. In this twisted construct, Khaled Nabhan, who held his murdered three-year-old granddaughter Reem—"the soul of my soul," as he called her—stiff in his arms and bid her goodbye with a loving, grief-stricken smile, is himself no longer important. What is important is whose fault you view his grief to be, and whether you believe his grief has been manufactured (or heightened, or accented, or whatever) for the eyes of the camera. In generalities we all profess that grief and loss of life are regrettable, but Khaled—the specific person and his specific incident—is only permitted to be a point on the spectrum, contextual-izable and dismissible.

The dismissal of the violence against us is not a by-product of the spectrum, but its purpose. The construct is designed to cheapen; it makes the bodies not a horrifying, sobering end point, but fodder to start a debate.

Any body in our inventory of bodies is likewise subject to similar deconstruction, equally debateable, and thus impossible to consider as part of a murderous design or trend. It is a tactic of domination that our bodies may not, even in their death, be given the grace of honesty about the horror that befell them. The exceptionalism of Israel, the spoiled infant of the exceptionalism of America, is such that its dead are forever mourned lugubriously and without qualification, while for our dead there is always enough qualification and debate to make you forget to mourn them at all.

I used to think the cheapness of Palestinian bodies is clearest when Israel kills a body that *isn't* Palestinian, especially if that body belongs to one of the privileged nationalities, the ones we know without having to name them. In those cases, there is a difference in the way the bodies are received. In September 2024, the Israeli army shot Ayşenur Ezgi Eygi, an American activist, as she was protesting in the West Bank. This time the body did not belong to a *fake* American like the journalist Shireen Abu Akleh, whom Israel killed in 2022 with no consequences. Abu Akleh, we all understood, was American only in quotation marks; she was really a Palestinian with an American passport. Eygi, on the other hand, was not beset by Palestinian blood in her veins. This time, the feeling went, Israel will be held to account for what it has done.

On its own, our anticipation of a differing treatment speaks to how ingrained in us is the cheapness of Palestinian lives. Maybe it comes from an understanding of the world's hypocrisy, and craving any opening to stem the murderous impunity. People expected an official condemnation by the US government, in-depth investigative articles about Eygi's murder, and an official memorial perhaps. I wasn't so sanguine, but I did think some American official would at least promise some cursory investigation. It turns out even I had aimed too high. There were a few articles reporting the fact of Eygi's death, many questioning whether Israel committed it. But there was no response from the State Department, no official call for an investigation, no in-depth pieces, and decidedly no major outcry from any news organizations. Eygi's activism for Palestinians had made her body cheap too, no matter how many times the words "from Seattle" were installed next to her name by people desperate for a consequence, any consequence. The cheapness of Palestinian bodies had become a communicable disease.

Around the same time, an Israeli-American man was found dead in the tunnels underneath Gaza after having spent ten months as a hostage. The American president released a statement about him on the same day.

An early sign of the catastrophic nature of Israel's assault was when we started talking about Gaza's civil registers. These are the records of the existence of people, their names, families, and properties. As the weeks piled up, we heard reports that whole Palestinian families had been wiped from the registers. For each of these families, that meant the family name no longer belonged to a living person in Gaza; all who carried it had been exterminated. It meant one less unit of collective rootedness to the land, the bloodline having been drained from the living to seep into the warred-over soil. I thought about how our families often have roots dating back hundreds of years—including my own family, whose members can recite by heart the names of ancestors spanning generations. And yet for families in Gaza, *this* was the year that extinguished them altogether.

One after the other, dozens of families kept getting wiped, at pace. Until one day, we learned that Israel simply destroyed the Gaza civil registry itself, thus killing two birds with one stone. Now the families don't exist, and neither does our accounting of them.

A tragedy ancillary to the human cost of the genocide is the loss of family histories. Most families the world over do not feature a historian, or a writer, or a poet, or a diarist, or a filmmaker, or a documentarian, or any kind of official record keeper. Their stories are kept alive by kin, by daughters and sons and aunts and uncles and cousins, speaking to each other over cups of tea or on the phone. *Oh, you didn't know that these two, whose wedding is tomorrow, have had eyes for each other since they were eight years old? Well it's true, my dear, and we all knew they'd end up together.* But these stories, ephemeral in the air in which they're spoken but enduring in the memories and imaginations of their holders and those who listen to them—those stories are gone when families are gone.

My family is one of the lucky ones. It has a record keeper, of sorts, unworthy and imperfect though I may be.

My ancestors on both sides were survivors of the Nakba. The Zionist gangs that infiltrated Palestine terrorized both sets of my grandparents out of their lands and homes in 1948. Unlike many thousands of Palestinians who perished that year, they escaped with their lives. Their newfound refugeehood took them on a tour of degradation through various Arab states. From the ones that limited them to refugee camps and prevented them from taking a job, to the ones that took their papers and compelled them into military service, to the ones that gave them citizenship but offered no work or prospects. They spent a decade like this, traversing with their freshly cheapened bodies the map lines over which Sykes and Georges-Picot once nodded at each other in approval.

Eventually, my grandparents stumbled their way to Kuwait in the 1950s, when it was still a British colonial protectorate. There they settled. (There they settled *for good*, is what I wrote before backspacing, having forgotten for a moment the delusion that is permanence for the likes of us.) Kuwait was somewhat less degrading than the rest. In that barely populated but outlandishly wealthy land, the well-educated could always find good jobs. Palestinians, for all their travails, rarely let themselves go uneducated. My mother was a chemistry teacher and my father was a paediatrician. Our family prospered, fashioning a life that on the surface felt warm with relative safety.

But it was a life that was circumscribed in decisive ways. Our statelessness had become a standard feature:

the national law was that we and our children could never be citizens, regardless of being born there, or how much we contributed to society. That meant that we could also never own property; only citizens could do that. Our residency was always required to be renewed, and forever revocable at a bureaucrat's whim.

Basic facts like these begat other oppressions. We could never forget that we were exiles.

I recall there were little prisons everywhere in our lives. There were houses we weren't allowed to live in. There were jobs we were not permitted to aspire to. There were countries that we saw in glossy magazines, but which our documents would not let us enter. There were things I could not say to my classmates at school, if they were from that privileged class of people called Kuwaiti, or those who had citizenships of any kind. There were crimes it would have been futile to report, depending on who the perpetrators were and whom they perpetrated against. There were social niceties that had to be observed, except that the consequence of not observing them was not a social ostracization but a physical one.

I learned about these boundary lines from the person who took them most seriously: my father. He made me feel them so acutely not just because he was the one who most often enforced the prisons in our family's life, but also because it seemed to me that he, of all people, should be the least troubled by limits, or beset with fear.

I am careful to say this not out of pride or even love, but to give a dead man his due: Ahmad Teebi was a giant in our family.

From my vantage point growing up as a child, the most salient thing about him was that he embodied that timeless holy grail of the migrant: He was a doctor. He obtained his medical degree from Cairo University in the early 1970s, the first (and to this day, the only) one in the family to do so. For the son of refugees, the achievement conferred on him a certain gravitas, and a mandate to live up to it. If he felt the pressure, it did not often show during my childhood in Kuwait. In a culture where consanguineous marriage was often used to improve familial bonds, my father found his way into the field of genetics. His research specialization was dysmorphology, a line of work that involves some of the most visually gut-wrenching of human conditions: congenital birth defects, almost uniformly untreatable. I remember once or twice I snuck into his office, which was forbidden to the family due to its graphic contents. It was littered with clinical photos and slides from his field trips to faraway locations, together with hand-scrawled notes with words like polydactyly, hypertelorism, nondisjunction. For a child, it was a disquieting menagerie. I remember having this thought: Anyone can muster the courage to be a surgeon and cut up people's skin and organs knowing they do so to help them, but who has the stomach to witness what bodily affronts had been ordained for people only to inform them, *There is nothing I can do for you*?

My father was the eldest of seven children, and from his youth he was their linchpin. As they scattered across the world, Ahmad was the fulcrum of familial connection and trust. A sister would call to ask how her other siblings were, because she knew that he would know. A brother, afraid for his money from his own appetites, would call to ask if my father might take some capital and invest on his behalf. It was an article of faith among them that Ahmad knew what was best, and that he would act on it.

His personality assisted with his mantle. He was gregarious and abidingly social, with a voice that reverberated across rooms. If he told a joke, he laughed and laughed at it until everyone else had no choice but to join in his laughter, whether due to mirth or oppression. If you entered a crowded room to look for my father, you'd not have to look long: everyone's heads were already turned in that direction. Belying his affability was the authority we felt in his presence, underpinned by an imperiousness that made him difficult to defy.

In 1973, Ahmad was finishing up his medical studies in Cairo. While he was there, his father, Said (my grandfather, after whom I was named), would sometimes send Ahmad newspapers from Kuwait to keep him apprised of the local goings-on. Back then, the newspapers annually published a list of all the high school graduates, together with pictures of the highest performers, ranked. You scanned the lists because in a country as small as Kuwait you might recognize some of the last names, and if you did, you should call and congratulate the family on their offspring's success. (The lists of high achievers were often cramped with Palestinians dying to prove their worth with overperformance.) In his final year, as Ahmad leafed through *Al Qabas*, he saw a photo of a beautiful young woman, with feathered hair and a knowing, elusive smile. All he knew about her was that photo, and that her marks ranked her first in the country, with an eye-popping average score.

His fingers still smudged from the newsprint, he called his father back in Kuwait. Baba, I am almost finished with medical school, he said. Can we see if I can marry this woman from the newspaper? Do you think she would take me?

She, and her family, took him, although not before some early trepidation and resistance from my mother. To her eyes, this new Dr. Ahmad looked too much like her beloved older brother Sulayman, whom she could not bear the thought of replacing in her life. But she agreed eventually, finding in the resemblance a sign of her nascent love.

In the wedding pictures, my father is wearing a velvet suit, hair combed over his balding head. On his arm is my mother, vivacious in her long-sleeved, filigreed white dress, the elegant pride of her family. My father looked powerful, and happy.

I pile together the various parts of my father's life to understand the total of the load he carried. He had the responsibility of parents who gloried in him. Siblings who connected through him. My mother who took him as her partner, and his young children who were dependent on him. Then there was his newly acquired position of societal rank and enmeshment, which he could not permit himself to relinquish or miscarry, as a historical matter as much as a personal one.

As I consider him now, these responsibilities clarify the importance of the prisons to him. His prisons sometimes reflected real, written-down laws, and sometimes reflected realities that didn't need laws. Some of the prisons were made of my father's abundance of caution. However these boundaries originated, he was extraordinarily careful not to cross them. His fear of the consequences, to him and especially to his dependents, coloured how he lived.

For my father, the way to account for the precariousness of our lives was to give as much as he could to our new environment, and be content with whatever it gave in return. And why shouldn't we be content? Our prisons were not *actual* prisons, with barred windows and cruel wardens. We were far from the cells in which Israel chucks Palestinians, without charge or accusation, with the casualness of a hair toss. We were not even in an open-air prison from which leaving is barred, where a fast-food meal has to be smuggled across borders through secret passages. By comparison, things were rosy for us in Kuwait. There, unlike in the West, most everyone you met sympathized with Palestinians. They told you they understood your plight, and shook their heads in sorrow at the thought of what you must have gone through. You felt the pain in the intensity of the prayers they said for you in your presence. Underneath our skins and beyond our passports, our plight is a collective one, they told you, even as they start businesses while you are permitted to do no more than be their employee. They understood that you were a victim of a massive historical tragedy, which they believed would inevitably be corrected. Time will pull the bloody threads of tragedy out of your lives and transform it into a heroic narrative instead. You will need everyone's help for that to happen, they said, and we are ready, whenever the time comes. They agreed with you that this or that hypocrite ruler of this or that country had betrayed you, and made your journey even more difficult. They may have even agreed, in whispers, that it was possible *our* ruler had not been as helpful as he could be, or perhaps he just has a different approach to helping—a longer view, or a more strategic one, the wisdom of which you will see in good time. On the whole you had to concede that your life was pretty good, all things considered. Everyone loves you, the way you speak, the food you make, how bright you are, and how useful. They are, truly, your brothers and sisters.

The reality was that after my grandparents left Palestine's newly redrawn borders, they and all their subsequent lineage were suddenly barred from going back. The new Zionist masters had made our homeland unavailable to us on a permanent basis. Our new country of refuge, then, with how it's taken us in, must be honoured and respected. The need for self-preservation, together with an Arab sense of propriety and deference to hosts, mandated it. So what if our new society had a set of rules that forever marked our difference and inferiority? We had no choice but to live with it.

The first rule in my father's prisons was to minimize any talk of politics or history. He fed us children the basic facts, and no more. I grew up knowing that we were Palestinian, and that we were unjustly displaced, but not the history or the specifics of that displacement, not even my family's own history. What knowledge I had came from TV programs, or the official curriculum, when it veered in that direction. The 1948 massacres at Deir Yassin, Lydda, and Tantura were not things my father recounted to me. I became aware of them on my own, via stray references in magazine articles. I caught wind of the more recent Sabra and Shatila massacre on the car radio once, as part of some retrospective program that my father hurriedly turned off.

My father's philosophy—which I gathered but was never told—was that talking about such things only brought about thoughts and desires that children cannot be trusted with. Ours was a just cause, but you never knew who to trust, or when talking about such things will hurt you. That kind of knowledge requires nuance. Children could not be entrusted with nuance; it could barely be entrusted to adults. So we were given silence.

I was barred from watching the evening news (although I sometimes caught glimpses of the nearly as disturbing Egyptian melodramas that preceded it). Whenever there was mention of a casualty in the West Bank or Gaza, whether it was brought up by a guest or by the television, my father motioned me far away. Go, go, to your room. I don't know if he was sheltering me from associating with victimhood, from the notion of death itself, or from the fact that death is happening to people so proximate to us, whose precariousness was very like ours.

Growing up, our family's flat was a community hub. It seemed like we had company over three or four times a week at least. Mostly other Palestinian families, fellow physicians from my father's work, or fellow teachers from my mother's. My father insisted that I sit with the other men, but my presence was contingent on not saying anything foolish or dangerous. If, during one of those visits, I took my adult playacting too far and opened my mouth to express a viewpoint, my father would start with his glares and manufactured coughs. I was sensitive to these public reprimands. Soon, I felt it was safer to bar myself from speaking. Who could trust what I might say, or think?

Sometimes—not often—after our guests had gone away, my father would gesture at the rationale behind his prodding guidance. I just want what's best for you, he'd say. I want people to think you're smart and mature. That you are stable.

I didn't parse his words too carefully back then. At that age, my father's attitude felt like an indictment of me as a person. I am not trustworthy, I am not knowledgeable, I am not smart or measured enough in my actions, I am not fit to be with others. It never occurred to me that it might be a symptom of his own debilitations.

Fear left to its own devices runs amuck. It becomes a way of life. It infiltrates. Our bodies felt to me like they were threatened everywhere. There was no safety. It didn't help that my father was a veteran of numerous health troubles, including his first kidney transplant in his twenties. He knew in his flesh the potential consequences of not acting in self-preservation. But his fearful impulses extended far and wide. If a glass of water spilled, my father could not last a minute without requiring it to be wiped, for fear that someone might slip and fall on it. Bodies of water were verboten, and his kids did not learn to swim until later in life. Running too fast in his presence meant an inevitable fall and had to be reprimanded. Once, I went outside to the courtyard of our apartment building and saw on the sidewalk a smattering of prescription pills, together with an open pill jar, near where our car was parked. Someone must have spilled them and not bothered to clean up. Eight years old or so at the time, I collected the pills one by one, reaching my fingers under the tires of cars and in the crevices of the asphalt. I dropped them all back in the jar and rushed inside to hand it to my father, worried that otherwise one of my younger siblings might mistake a pill for candy and pop it in their mouth. My father rewarded me with a week's worth of loud praise for the maturity and care that I exhibited. I don't think my high school graduation had him bragging to people as much as this incident did.

My father's fear of harm led my mother to dismiss some of his concerns as the sign of a mwaswas—an Arabic word that has its origins in a quasi-religious vein, describing someone who has been whispered to by Satan. I was fascinated that my rational father could be gripped by doubts of a cosmic, almost superstitious nature. Being mwaswas seemed a complete explanation for erratic behaviour—it was a condition beyond one's control, a paralysis of fears one had to submit to since it came via powers of a higher order than them. I didn't understand it this way back then, but it must have been handy to manage trauma by reducing it to a mere bedevilment.

The defining example of my father's mwaswas state was his conduct around balconies. In a childhood spent ensconced in a series of apartments, balconies represented a delicious liminal space for me. Between the heat that consumed your flesh outside, and the lonely, thunderous shoves of the air-conditioning inside, the balcony felt like the best of two harsh worlds. The thought of standing on a balcony and gazing at the world of swirling dust, weaving BMXs, and parked Cressidas and Caprice Classics—as a child, such power felt almost royal.

Except my father strictly forbade any children to venture anywhere near a balcony. The children could get between the spindles (even if our bodies were too large), or they could hop over it off some platform (even if there was no platform in sight) and plummet into the depths below (one or two storeys). Even if we stayed some distance away, he'd still be fixated on the matter, checking in our direction every few seconds. It became a sort of family mania: if there was a balcony, each family member would warn the other to stay far away or suffer the consequences. Sometimes a less cautious elder, most often his father-in-law, would prevail upon my father that I or one of my siblings could survive a moment sitting on a chair on the balcony. My father would be forced to concede, his anxieties having to take second place to the rules of propriety. But the whole time he would eye us like a hawk.

To me, the fear that motivated my father to shelter me from knowledge of historical massacres is of a kind with the fear that made him scramble, falling over furniture and things, when he saw me stride in the direction of a balcony.

He could not imagine a scenario in which our bodies were not in danger.

And now, I couldn't trust my own hands around the staircase of my house.

The contractor who came, in December 2023, to give me a quote about walling it up was a Syrian man. He scratched his head in confusion when I told him what I wanted. He asked me flatly why I'd want to ruin such a beautiful feature of the house.

I felt stupid. I must've seemed to him like some disturbed character from Poe. I explained about my visions. I said I was so very tired of feeling fear. I'd had enough.

He smiled. Ah yes, you are mwaswas, he said, using my mother's word for my father's hysterical phobias.

He added: But I advise you to not make decisions right now, habeebi, it's too soon.

What did he mean it's too soon?

He said: Look, the fighting will stop, and we will all stop having these visions.

I wanted to explain to him that my problem started in 2022, predating Israel's war on Gaza. But as I said it, I had a shiver of recognition. I remembered.

Before October 7, Israel had launched many cyclic assaults on Gaza. The last one was two years before, in 2021. Israel's warplanes had bombed many buildings, reducing them to rubble and fire. Children had fallen from these buildings too. I followed these events every day on my phone and my satellite TV. They had happened almost a year before we moved into our new house.

My visions were not imaginings after all, they were re-enactments. My mind was effecting upon my daughter's body horrors that happened to other people's daughters, other people's sons. It turned out that I had inherited the fears of my father, just not in the genetic way I suspected.

At least I could pinpoint how I got my bodily fear. My father has been dead for many years now, so I cannot ask him about his.

I turned to my mother. When I asked her how her husband got like that, she said: *his* father taught him the fear.

My grandfather Said Teebi was a Palestinian like the many Palestinians who became small details in the colonial expedition of fabricating a home for the Jewish people. Said was from a village called Salama, some three miles east of the glittering coastal city of Jaffa. My grandmother Nima Owainat was from Qalqilya, a bit farther to the east.

Nima had lived near Jaffa most of her life, and so she did not have the distinctive Qalqilyan accent that rendered the rounded *qaf* sound into a hard *kaf*. Still, Said sometimes teased Nima about that accent, calling her the girl from *Kalkeelyeh*.

In 1948, the couple were still newlyweds, really. They'd married the year before, after Said had come back from Al-Azhar University, the famed Islamic studies institute in Cairo where he took his degree. He had already started teaching in a neighbouring school, while Nima was busy establishing their small home.

From the moment Said and Nima married, they never used their first names. Instead, they called each other by the name of the child they planned to have: Ahmad. Said called his wife Um-Ahmad, and Nima called her husband Abu-Ahmad. Mother of Ahmad, and father of Ahmad. It was their demure way of planting between them the seed of familiarity, a union in the form of a future child.

And now Nima was pregnant.

Early in that year, people were afraid that the Zionist militias would come to Salama any day. Said sometimes got his hands on the *Falastin* newspaper. There were articles that told of ships filled with Jews from Europe arriving on Palestine's shores every week. There were even more alarming articles about clashes with Zionists in various Palestinian towns, and about massacres whose horror could scarcely be believed.

Said learned about what the militias had done in Deir Yassin to the south, and what they had done in Tantura to the north. In Deir Yassin, the Zionist gangs took the town's citizens out of their homes, and, for an audience, trotted them through the Old City of Jerusalem. Some they executed near the quarry, others they took back to the village to execute there. Women and children were not exempt; they numbered half of those killed. It was not just a massacre, it was an announcement.

To my grandfather Said, this massacre, and others like it, were not yet the bloody history that my father would end up shielding us from. They were current events.

Some men from Said's village had already fled, believing they'd be back in a few weeks, once the Zionists were quelled for good. Other men were preparing to resist. Salama was populated mainly by lifelong farmers. Most didn't have firearms, although with the imminent threats, they were trying to obtain some.

Said and Nima did not want to leave. Salama was their home, and their families were all there. Still, Nima's pregnancy was already advanced, and Said had never touched a rifle in his life. The young couple knew that some people went north to Lebanon. Others went east to Transjordan.

That country, albeit impoverished and resource-deficient, would later hand out citizenship to any Palestinians who crossed over, part of a deal it struck with the Zionists. Others still went west, and jumped into the sea, letting the boats choose where they went. How could the destination matter, really, when every destination was not home?

Said and Nima decided that if they had to go, they would go south, toward Egypt. Said favoured it because it was familiar. He knew Cairo bustled with life and opportunity. He dreaded the heat but at least he had acquaintances there, and could find his way around its tight alleys. It could be a good way station for a short while.

Said and Nima finally left in the middle of summer. Already nearby Jaffa was being demolished, with the Manshiya neighbourhood especially resembling a project of gray destruction. Nima was no longer moving well. Said, slight but determined, held her hand, and let her arm rest on his shoulder. They took the journey by foot, along the coast. The walk was slow, and the sun did not spare them.

As I look at a map of Palestine from 1947 published by *National Geographic*, and I confirm it with countless more detailed maps in Arabic that I scoured from archives, I can see the names of towns my grandparents probably passed on their way: Beit Dajan, Isdud, El Majdal, El Jora, Khan Yunis. But I do not know where they stopped, or what they did at the stops. I don't know if some motorist saw Nima's belly and took mercy, letting the couple ride in their car or on the flatbed of their truck. My grandmother was voluble, and quick to laughter, so maybe that helped. Was there at least a bus, or a horse, or a donkey for part of the way? At night, did they sleep on the streets? Did they find hospitable houses?

Said and Nima both passed away before I was an adult; I had no chance to ask them. Their story's features are blurry to me. The vanishing of stories is not a side effect of displacement, it is a primary objective. The stories, untied from the land, dissociate and dissolve.

Finally, the couple reached Rafah, the border town at the southernmost tip of Gaza. They crossed what looked like a makeshift checkpoint at the border.

Once in Egypt, Said was surprised. Egypt was no longer treating him the way it did when he was a visiting student, just a year or so before. Back then, he had been allowed to enter, go anywhere he liked, find a residence, and pursue an education. Now, the Egyptian soldiers told him he could move no farther than the refugee camp set up on the Egyptian side of Rafah. He had exited Palestine only to find himself in this place that was neither his home, however blighted by colonizers bringing war, nor a non-home with safety and opportunity. It was something in between, with none of the features of a reasonable life.

Here are the tents, the Egyptian soldiers said, you may take one if you wish.

Said and Nima laid down their blankets on the floors of

their tent. Nima settled in a corner, relieved to be off her feet. She loosened the knot in the bottom of her cursory veil and let her cheeks breathe. Her feet and legs were enormous with bloat. Neither of them had eaten a proper meal in days. She had many aches and pains, but she tried her best to forget them. There were no medical services anyway.

Said spent most of his days in the Rafah camp searching for food, and Nima cooked what he brought in borrowed pots.

For the life of him, Said still could not understand why he wasn't permitted to go farther into Egypt, to the places he knew and understood. He was the same person he was the previous year, the same blood and mind. But now that he was a refugee, it was like he was from a different planet. He felt like his worth had been slashed to nothing.

From what I remember of my grandfather, he would have likely argued daily with whatever Egyptian soldier he could find. *We only need to venture into Cairo temporarily. We need a place to live until things settle down, and some work so I can provide for my unborn child—my first one. Are you aware that I am a scholar from Al-Azhar? What do you have that I don't have, soldier?*

Later, in private, one of the soldiers would come to Said offering to spirit him farther into Egypt, for a fee. But Said was young and destitute. All the money he had was not nearly enough to take the soldier up on his offer.

Only days after they had arrived in Rafah, Nima went into labour. Her baby, Ahmad, the one she'd been dreaming of, was coming. She was alone, her husband having gone on one of his errands. I don't know what time of day this happened. Their flimsy tent had made it so that any time of the day was the same, exposed to the elements as they were. Nima's labour progressed with alarming quickness. She screamed for Said, over and over. Some women from neighbouring tents came to coach her through it. The soldiers shooed them away—*Go back to your own tents.*

When Said arrived, he panicked at the sight. It was too soon; they had not yet prepared for the delivery. It was Said's turn to scream: *Are there any doctors? Anyone who can deliver this baby? Please!* But he knew the answer. There were no doctors for the camps. There were not supposed to be any. He ran to a soldier. The soldier—and this was a familiar sight—shrugged.

Actually, I don't know if it happened exactly that way. But I do know this: Said, my grandfather, a schoolteacher in his early twenties, was forced to deliver his first baby himself. The women who came to the tent had brought warm water but declined to help more. They had glimpsed that the umbilical cord was wrapped around the baby's neck, and it made them afraid to do anything. So it was left to Said. He was terrified. He pulled the baby. He did not know any better. In his panic he kept pulling, urgently, strongly. Nima pushed and cried. Said pulled.

The baby seemed to emit a cry. But from what Said could see of him in the tent, the baby was blue. Talk to me, son. Talk to me. The baby did not answer, not with a cry nor with a breath. The baby was dead.

Said looked at the baby for a long time before letting go. The nature of his new reality had probably not crystallized yet. But this moment, which he will rehash many times in the future, will be the one he comes back to. This moment when no one cared to help him, when his environment—this new nowhereland—seemed most arid and hostile, when he had suddenly become a different person, an unwanted, useless person, when he could not even bring his firstborn safely into the world.

I assume that's the moment when he began to distrust his hands, and himself. I assume that's when he began to fear.

Said buried the baby in the ground of the camp. He did not want to name the baby, but Nima insisted. She said she'd heard the baby cry, so the baby deserved a name, even if they could not bear to give it the name they had planned, Ahmad. Instead, they called the baby Jihad, a name signifying struggle. The struggle that was Nima's journey with the baby, and the new struggle that was now her and Said's lot in life.

A year later, Said and Nima had left their nightmare in Rafah and traveled to Beirut. There, Nima did give birth to a baby named Ahmad—my father. He was not Said and

Nima's firstborn, but he was their eldest, with six more to come.

But already in this young Palestinian family's life, this family that had *fled*, already there had been born a body and a fear.

– 2 –

Reclamation and Rebuilding

For our family, the death of baby Jihad in 1948 was the first time our bodies were laid to waste as a function of our Palestinianness. The years proved that Jihad was only the very leftmost side of a decades-long exponential curve of obliteration. The curve is crammed with children for data points. In September 2024, the Ministry of Health in Gaza published 649 pages' worth of names of Palestinians known to have been killed by Israel's assaults; the first fourteen of those pages were names of infants under a year old.

My grandfather Said buried a baby that day, but he also buried the story. The child suffocating in his inexpert hands felt like his fault. It was his fault for being a Palestinian, for not staying in Palestine, for choosing Egypt, for not knowing enough about delivering babies, for not organizing his words and cries in such a way as to make someone understand and help him. His displacement was, from its very beginning, a catastrophe of both historic and personal dimensions. More than just broken, he felt utterly humiliated.

In Kuwait, Said and his young family were away from the tents and inside brick and mortar. There were hospitals that offered medical care and delivered his children. But Said's knowledge that their bodies were threatened did not go away. Said was the first to create the prisons of what we can and can't say, how we can express ourselves and to whom. He enforced his rules with the timeless combination of stick and temper. My father accepted the prisons and perfected them, adding more and more, for both him and us.

Said and Nima spent all their forty years in Kuwait as refugees. They had a two-bedroom apartment where they raised their children. Their shorthand for having raised them well was their education: doctors, teachers, businessmen, aerospace engineers. But as a schoolteacher himself, Said was an employee in a government job. He knew that the looming of mandatory retirement came with a parting gift: the expiration of his work visa. No more lifelines at the renewals office. He was only welcome so long as his body was hale enough to provide services.

Instead of waiting to be forced to leave, my grandfather took his final risk. A relation in California had extended him and Nima the opportunity of a green card. America is an advertisement for security and prosperity, and its power is not in its ability to fulfill the advertised promises, but in our being captivated by the promotion itself. For my stateless grandparents, it was irresistible. The Palestinian passports they'd been born with had been rendered null and void by the enactment of the Israeli state. Now they were in grasp of some of the most potent papers in the world.

Said was sixty-five, and older than that sounds. I remember the cocktail of medications always rattling in the pockets of his blue-grey thawb. When he walked, he had the gait of someone hopping without leaving the ground. One of his index fingers was a stump. The children's grapevine, fed by a scarcity of facts, held that he'd caught a bullet in war, but in truth the injury was a civilian one: the work of a paper trimmer's blade. Nima was younger than Said, but aged even faster. She was disabled by her diabetes, her legs enormous and varicose. On the rare occasions she was on her feet, she lumbered with constant pain.

Said and Nima immigrated to America in the late 1980s, settling in San Diego. Soon after, Nima was in the throes of terminal disease. My father flew our family over to visit. But when it came down to it, it was still too much for him to let us children face death. I was twelve, but he sequestered me and my younger siblings for days at our relatives' house while he and my mother bid Nima farewell.

Later that same year we traveled to California again, this time to visit my now widowed grandfather. I remember a solitary armchair in his dank ground-floor apartment, Arabic newspapers piled on the side table. He was living life from pill to pill, timed like prayers. One of my uncles lived with him, and they bickered. Mostly my grandfather picked at his bald head from the aggravation of loneliness. This bright new land seemed an adventure he was not up to.

My family did not intend to stay in America. My parents, in their late thirties at the time, had excellent jobs back in Kuwait, where my father was close to a revered figure. By then, he'd already been awarded the country's top honour for a scientist, a lifetime-type of achievement that he captured before middle age. His success gave our family the luxury of an instrumentalist attitude toward America: get the papers if they will give them to you, but don't feel compelled to stay. Our time in Kuwait may have been capped like it was for my grandfather, but we *had* time. We'd only leave when we were ready. My father wanted to finally choose.

That summer we acted like tourists, not refugees. We went to the San Diego Zoo, my father wearing a neon-pink fanny pack below his belly pudge, my mother the archetype of a sporty hijabi in her knee-length shirt and oversized sunglasses. We went to Disneyland and Universal Studios. How wide were our eyes when we saw the machinery that helped E.T. and Elliott soar into the air on their bicycle. America, the land of flight. I remember that I had overpacked, hoping we'd get to stay somehow.

We visited my grandfather daily. Still practicing for adulthood per my father's instructions, I sat and listened to my parents conversing with him. Mostly they talked about papers. *What dates will we be eligible to apply for citizenship? Have we lined up the necessary materials and money? Who else can be brought over?* My grandfather's mind seemed occupied in its entirety by those papers that he intended to pass on like an heirloom.

Sometimes my grandfather asked me to go on walks near Balboa Avenue with him. He gripped my shoulder for support as he hopped in his usual way. I did not like these walks. He alternated between risqué jokes intended for me, and private mutterings to himself about the new society he was witnessing and judging: its bombast, sexuality, and speed. My English was poor but not as poor as his. I was the conduit between my grandfather and the world. I took change from shopkeepers and thanked them in a loud voice when he forgot or didn't bother.

When the conversation between us flagged, my grandfather recited a certain old verse. He had been repeating it for as long as I knew him, without needing an occasion.

He said it whether he was alone or with people, some-times with a twinkle in his eye and sometimes with sad-ness. It was a single satiric line by a fifteenth-century poet named Ali Ibn Sūdūn:

وفي الهيجاءِ ما جربت نفسي   ولكن في الهزيمة كالغــزالِ

I have not tried myself in war, but like a gazelle am I in defeat

To my young ears it was the best joke my grandfather ever told, and I did not tire of hearing it. So ludicrous to be beaten without even going to battle. It spoke to a loserness so acute that it couldn't be anything other than parody.

That I knew nothing of my grandfather's history meant that he could state this code for his tragedy freely. I never registered it as a mantra of the haunted.

Slaughter has been my main measure of Israel's destruc-tion in Palestine. But for the oppressor it's just the most final way to remove bodies, not the only one. The toolbox of oppression is deep with helpful indignities.

As the Gaza war began to unfold, Israel seemed to be making a point, for its audience of international allies, of directing Palestinians to scurry from one end of the Strip to the next. This was framed as a kindness: We would like the innocent to survive, so we give them a chance to leave the areas we will soon bomb. That the leaflets from the sky directing people to "safe zones" often funneled them to an ambush in those zones is only a grisly detail. It was a given that leaving was preferable to death. In just a few weeks the number of the internally displaced rose until it reached very near the total population of Gaza.

Forcible displacement leaves no part of life unchanged. A rich existence full of particularities and desires is erased. The breakfast you are used to having, or the professional improvement classes you take at night—they are gone without another thought. What seemed indispensable about your life is eliminated as a matter of course. Life becomes about elemental things: how to find shelter, how to find food, how to stay alive. I remember many videos of Gazans opening their aid packages of flour and sugar and jubilating: there will be bread tonight, they shouted, as if it were the height of opulence. Luxury was redefined so that it now included things that aren't even enjoyable, that do not feel like luxuries at all, like grieving for your dead, or for the loss of your previous way of living.

Our identities are not immune from the upheaval. A self-sufficient farmer who lived off their land is, without that land, someone who misses not just food or income but their way of thinking about themselves. A writer who lost their meticulously collected library doesn't even have the dignity of dwelling on it because it pales in comparison to the souls and livelihoods destroyed every day.

There is a flattening that happens in displacement. People may not lose their features, but their features lose significance in the circumstances. People become more alike. Their most elemental characteristics are the ones that matter: alive or dead, young or old, strong or weak. Basic human functions become high bars to clear. When forty or fifty people are forced to shelter together in an apartment—as happened many times in Gaza, when there were still such things as apartments—finding time to go to the bathroom becomes a problem in need of solving. People are rendered masses of needs, uniform in their basicness.

Even our connection to one another becomes utilitarian. The most important people you know become the people whose bakery has not been bombed, who have solar panels to charge your phone, who may be willing to take a trek with you to North Gaza to collect what food was left in your freezer before you had to flee. The main question between two people becomes: Can this person help me get through the day?

The loss of what is personal makes easier the oppressor's task of stripping their victims of humanity. Imaginations can no longer accommodate more than immediate necessities. In displacement, desire itself becomes unaffordable.

The best thing that we can conceive of in those circumstances is a return to what we had. We imagine, hard, what is newly unavailable to us, and it becomes what we pine for. Where before we took night classes so we could get a better job, or open a business, now all we want is a reset to even a poor facsimile of the life we led before the destruction. We collect all the pieces of that former life we can find, so that we may try to build it all back again. Displacement's most major trauma is the stunting of our dreams.

I was born in displacement, but on the whole, I was a happy child. If I try to remember my moments of greatest joy, I go back to the nights we spent at my maternal grandparents' place. My parents brought us there multiple times a week, like a default setting for our evenings. I used to think it was sweet that my father was happy to visit with his in-laws so much. Only much later did I realize he was doing it for his own sake.

My grandparents' apartment was located on the ground floor of a dun building, in a block filled with Palestinians and Egyptians in the Hawally area of Kuwait. My best friend during my childhood was my cousin Abed. We were born a few months apart, each of us the firstborn of close sisters. Abed and I often captained teams of our younger brothers and cousins to kick around a soccer ball in the building's outdoor common space. We'd clamour and fight about it until suppertime. Sometimes my grandmother cooked, but it was common for us to order takeout from Canary Restaurant, which everyone knew was the best place for Palestinian food. My young aunt Sanaa and I were often sent to pick it up, sacrificial lambs to Canary's long, impatient lineups. When we returned with the food, the place rose at attention. By then all my aunts and uncles would have arrived, and one of them would tear the bags open. Each plate received a dollop of hummus sheeted in golden olive oil, with two or three warm balls of falafel wobbling next to it. After supper, as the adults conversed, Abed and I went to the back room and schemed: our dreams were a weird melange of starting technology companies, publishing magazines, and founding theatre troupes. Every now and then, we barreled back to the grown-ups for their input, preferably adulatory, on our blueprints.

Nostalgia is the slyest form of self-deception, but those nights were heaven to me.

But I want to think of these nights now not through my own eyes, but through those of my father. Ahmad had married into a family of Palestinian refugees like his own, though that was the end of the similarities. His father-in-law Shaban was a swashbuckling figure, booming and decisive, who did not allow his life to feel like anything less than exactly what he wanted. With his strong jaw and pencil mustache, he had a majestic handsomeness—and was well aware of it. He had been a young citrus merchant in Jaffa, sending crates of oranges from his family's groves to Europe in exchange for shipments of Mercedes-Benz cars to resell in Palestine. In Kuwait he reinvented himself, starting a sweets shop where he sold gummy Arabic ice cream and candy floss. (As often as I could manage, I hung out in the attic of that shop like a sugar-addicted bat.) From the day Shaban met Ahmad, they struck up an admiring friendship seasoned with light, unidirectional provocation. I remember my father's happy chatter often being interrupted with sardonic opposition from Shaban, testing his son-in-law's mettle. When Ahmad got worked up and defensive, Shaban cackled and lowered his verbal sword.

But the person my father spent much of his time with was his mother-in-law, my grandmother Samiyeh. She was a diminutive woman, gentle as cotton. With her flamboyant husband around, she might have been easy to overlook, but my father made a point of seeking her company. Samiyeh would sit on the sofa and cross her legs at the ankles, rubbing her socked feet together. When the children were away in the back room, Ahmad plied her with questions. What was Palestine like before the Jews fought us? What was her village near Jerusalem like? What were their signature meals? How were the people and the landscape? In her soft, lilting voice, Samiyeh answered him.

Ahmad also asked her about the agony of the time after her family's expulsion, of her and Shaban's first years together in Beirut, where she gave birth to Ahmad's eventual wife, my mother. Samiyeh told him a story of how my mother, then four or so years old, once asked her for something to eat. But the cupboard was bare, and they had no money. Instead of explaining to her daughter the grim reality, Samiyeh said the problem was that she'd run out of matches to start the gas cooker. To Samiyeh, not having matches was just a happenstance, but not having food was a horror. And so she assigned her daughter busy work: if you can find a match, then I will cook. The girl looked and looked, to no avail. Bored, she went outside. An hour later, she came back with a dusty match she'd harvested from Beirut's streets, where some smoker must have tossed it. Samiyeh wept. Now what?

Ahmad devoured those stories. Where his father had withheld history for the pain and fear that it carried, Ahmad found in his mother-in-law someone who obliged his voraciousness. He compared what Samiyeh told him with the readings he'd done on his own, coming back to her for clarification and elaboration.

Maybe their relationship was helped by a shared avocation. Samiyeh was a sub-rosa poet. As she went about her day as a housewife, she sometimes stopped and wrote lines in pencil on tiny slips of paper, tucking them in the pockets of her housedress when she was done. Some of her compositions she read to select company, but the inner lining of those pockets was the main audience for most of her verses. That didn't bother Samiyeh. There were times the family played poetry recall games: someone would begin with a line or two from some legend of Arabic verse, and the next person must pick up the final letter of the verse to start the next quote. For her turn, sometimes my grandmother offered a verse unfamiliar to the rest of the family, prompting her husband to tut and chide her: No, no, Samiyeh, those lines are your own invention. Samiyeh answered: So is it not poetry for being mine?

Ahmad was less secretive about his compositions—some of them anyway. I remember him publishing in the local paper some quasi-didactic verses about quitting smoking, for example. But on one of my covert forays into my father's office I found a blue notebook, hanging together by a literal thread along its spine. It looked to be from before medical school, so his handwriting was still legible. Most of the verses I found there were about Palestine, specifically his father's hometown of Salama. The poems were resolute, even combative. My father named his enemies with clarity, and named the consequences for their transgressions on his family's land. They were filled with vows of defiance and steadfastness.

I recognized in these poems keystone values of Palestinian freedom fighters since the Nakba—but I did not recognize my father.

This person, who was careful not to speak too much of Palestine, had been hiding an intense obsession with it. In the poems he referenced rifles, when I knew he'd never come in contact with one. He referenced leading a defence of his village, a defence that would have been decades late. Even Salama, the recurring star of his poems, was a star in soft focus. The town was garbed in my father's love and longing, but it had no real features or specifics, because he had never seen it.

I found it hard to understand why he wrote these poems. My father was never going to go to Palestine brandishing a sword or rifle. Even if he'd had the intention, he had no documents to permit him to go, even on a visit. He was also by constitution a tender person, and squeamish at the sight of blood or guts. Especially when I revisited the poems as an adult, they read like false mythologies about himself, and a little ridiculous. Was he not conscious of himself as he wrote them?

I don't know if my father discussed his old nationalistic poems with my grandmother. I was too busy in the back room making plans for the future with my cousin Abed. But I wonder if, perhaps, in the space between two people for whom flights of the mind are important, there was room for feeling and saying things that may sound ridiculous, room for the vulnerability of imagining.

In parallel with the war of extermination in Gaza, there always loomed a big question: Who can take the Palestinians? The Western world pondered this question in earnest editorials and special TV segments. Meanwhile Israel, with and through America, conducted secret negotiations with its Arab neighbours on this matter. Why can't Jordan, already filled with people of Palestinian origin, take them? There is so much space in Sinai, so why can't Egypt open its wall and let some Gazans languish in the desert for a spell? What about those belligerent Lebanese—if Hezbollah cared enough to militarily confront Israel, shouldn't they at least accept more refugees? When the American presidency turned over in 2025, the forcible displacement of the Palestinians evolved from a discreet but delicious discussion indulged in by Western operatives and pundits to an official state declaration of intended criminality by Israel's greatest ally.

Nineteen forty-eight was the first time Israel displaced Palestinians from their lands in mass numbers. Back then it was clear that, in the West's eyes, the Palestinians were, as Edward Said put it, just miscellaneous Arabs. The conception flattened Palestinians into masses of people *like* them, which was close enough. The displaced are not a *particular* people, they are an *any* people. If people witness the disposableness of their bodies enough times, perhaps they come to consider their national consciousness disposable too. In such a case they could be shuffled around at the will of the colonizer. Like an Etch A Sketch, all you had to do was shake all the tiny particles vigorously and the picture would clean up.

More than three-quarters of a century on, nothing has changed.

To the West, Palestinian resettlement is akin to the big novel project a failed writer circles back to whenever they feel in their life a bubble of crisis or gumption. When it came up during the course of the genocide, it was obvious to the West that the best solution for their "Palestinian problem" was one that did not involve them staying in Gaza. Israel's right to invade the land, and take whatever parts of it they wished, was never disputed; the only issue was how to handle its irritating occupants. Palestinian agency didn't come up. The imperialist worldview is such that the turbaned and hijabed boogeypeople of the Western imagination are incapable of making good decisions for themselves, so they must not be permitted to try.

Displacement is, to the colonizer, convenient. The bodies are eliminated but the kill counts do not rise. The colonizer's hands are already bloody, but it's nice to reduce the dirty work if you can swing it. In their calculus there is also a moral neutrality to displacement, with gusts to moral good even. It's only a historical accident that *these* people were on *those* lands to begin with. Certainly, they are not connected to it with anything approaching the weight of biblical scripture. Their desire to stay on the land, the thinking goes, is not defensible or even relevant. So long as they can be put elsewhere, their bodies intact, what is the issue?

The best part is that, as soon as a refugee is created, they are by definition someone else's problem. The exit is one-way, and permanent. The clean severing of that obligation must be satisfying. The history of a person on the land is rendered meaningless because their greatest leverage—their occupancy—is eliminated.

Now, it's true that some or other countries must be found, or prevailed upon, to take the refugees. Usually certain states will volunteer out of some sense of international comity, or maybe as a backdoor favour, for public relations, or even from kindness or pity. Yet in their new land the refugee is not only a stranger, with all the difficulties that entails, with all the necessary rebuilding and the phantom limb of their lost country. Their life is also now saddled with conditions. Refuge countries have expectations that the refugee must satisfy, under threat of expulsion or irretrievable failure—expectations that other citizens do not have. While on your own land your existence was a given, as a refugee you must justify it. You have to prove your value in a way that can be measured and evaluated. And you have to disclaim your past, your sense of belonging to a prior place, as that sort of thing only hampers you from proving your worth.

The liminality that is the real home of refugees is a place with immutable features, ones that define their existence and imprint upon them forever.

In 1948 some countries offered refuge, however imperfect, to Palestinians exiled from Palestine. In the wake of the Gaza war, things were different. Just a couple of years before, Ukrainian refugees, glowing in whiteness, found no shortage of destinations for their emigration. But Palestinians, primarily duskier and Muslim on top of their objectionable base identity, were universally rejected. The states that egged on the genocide in Gaza like the rabid cronies of a bully—all of them withdrew their names from consideration for the taking of refugees. Even Canada, which offered a token number of spots, saddled them with conditions that rendered refuge all but impossible to secure in practice.

To the Gazans that had yet to be killed, the world said: Even the small shred of salvation you might seek in fleeing the only land you've ever known—even that, we will not grant you.

The summer that my family spent touring California in 1990 was our last happy time for years.

We had planned to return to Kuwait with enough time left in the summer for us children to get settled in before school started in the fall. On the day we were supposed to board our plane back—August 2, 1990—we received news that the flight was canceled. Hours before, Saddam Hussein had sent his army down Highway 80 from Basra to invade Kuwait.

I remember my parents watching the news in disbelief. My father stood with both hands on his head. My mother sat at the edge of the sofa, her hand covering her mouth, repeating, Is this real?

Everything we had in life was in that tiny smudge of geography near the tip of the Persian Gulf. Most of our relatives and friends were there. Our furniture, our bank accounts, our photo albums, our books of science and literature. All of it was now under control of the raiding Iraqi army.

We were stranded in California. For my parents it must have felt like they had fallen into an abyss. Our lives were reset. Our bodies had once again become precarious, this time in a confusing, Western-flavoured way. Were we supposed to feel lucky or unlucky? Was it better if we were in our homes in a war zone, or that we were in America, very far from home?

We worried about our family that remained in Kuwait— my aunts and uncles, and their kids. Trying to call them became a daily mission. I remember once aching to wrest the phone from my mother's hand as she talked to her sister. I wanted to say a couple of words to my cousin.

But my parents had immediate concerns of their own, most of them financial. The only things we now owned were whatever we happened to bring on our vacation. The cash we had on hand had already almost run out. When it was clear the conflict would be prolonged, my parents realized they had to find jobs. But their educations were no longer the assets they had been, their qualifications unrecognized in this new place. Stripped of its relationship to place, even knowledge can become worthless.

It wouldn't get better with time. Months later, after the US restored Kuwait to Kuwaiti rule—at the cost of dozens of billions of dollars, and the permanent installation of several US air bases—Palestinian residents were shunned. The Palestinian leadership at the time had not favoured America's intervention in the conflict, and the Kuwaitis reacted by making Palestinians persona non grata once they regained control of the country. Our family could not go back. The country that had accepted my grandparents' knowledge and entrepreneurship, and my father's grand achievements, was now done with us. Nearly 400,000 Palestinian residents of Kuwait were deported by 1991.

It's easy to smear Kuwait with the stain of this sin. The kindness it had purported to show Palestinians had apparently been so conditional that it did not survive one unfavourable political position. But I do not wholly fault that country. The original sin will always belong to the Zionists. That none of the Arab countries were generous to their Palestinian refugees is something for their conscience, but we should never have needed their generosity. We did not fall from the sky and onto their land, without address or home. This latest displacement had as its progenitor our original displacement from Palestine.

In the final analysis, my family was robbed of the chance to choose. The groundwork that my grandfather Said laid to put us in a position to get American passports was no longer a luxury to be accessed later if needed; it was now the only thing that could keep us in a country, any country.

The following years were a morass of uncertainty and destitution. Even though we were in the same America in which we vacationed, the luxury of complaining about the lines at Universal Studios now felt like a vestige of a past life. Our concerns became compacted: How can we stay? If we stay, how do we eat? Every last penny left from our vacation money was to be watched over. My father, proud and until very recently well-off, now had to ask his younger siblings for loans. I knew this hurt him because not a day went by that I didn't hear him worry about the funds he'd accepted, how he can pay them back, and whether what he took would even be enough. We called whoever we knew that still lived in Kuwait to try to retrieve for us things from our old flat—some albums, some poetry books, some jewelry.

We moved into a small mobile home in a rural part of Sacramento. We all slept on the floor, each in a corner of the house. My parents struggled to resurrect some semblance of their careers. My mother supported us, getting a job as a lab technologist, for the first time tasting in person American racism and sexism in her workplace. My father refused to resign himself to a job as a taxi driver or a gas station clerk, as some of our displaced relatives had. Those seemingly temporary fixes felt to him like lifelong albatrosses in disguise. Instead, he worked to pass qualification exams, one by one. This proud man, who had already achieved much in his life, had to prove that he could speak English first, so that he could then apply to do a medical residency at an American hospital like a junior physician.

As a twelve-year old, my problems did not feel as large as those of my parents. But now and then, as I walked back from my school, invariably alone, I wondered: Will I ever see my best friend—my cousin Abed—again?

One of the most frustrating aspects of displacement is how much it tethers you to your current reality. That a refugee is set back in their life is obvious. But in the intervening time between the displacement and the rebuilding, you become hostage to the reality of your precariousness. You are not at liberty to dream beyond it, because your greatest ambition is to somehow lessen your precariousness, to feel more secure. Even that often seems unachievable.

Reality is the nightmare of dreams. There is a sense in which the work of imagining at a grand scale is a product of luxury. We are always dreaming of something, but the scope of what we dream is restricted by how free we are to imagine it. I mean free broadly, but I also mean it in a stricter sense—do we have the free time? Those who have the luxury of not being besieged by their moment are in a better position to imagine very different future lives. The person working fifteen-hour days trying to not get evicted is not at luxury to think deeply about what they may do once they are out of that stage. That stage does not feel like a stage, it feels like the whole world. They are more likely to think only of the next step, because the next step feels monumental.

Worse, in displacement the next step is often one that you had already taken many years before. In America, my father became very tightly tethered to the new reality of his world. His drive to rebuild was obsessive. He passed his qualification exams, then redid his residency and fellowship, this time in their American varieties. He took positions at Yale, then at McGill, and then at the University of Toronto, conducting research at the universities and working as a clinician at their affiliated hospitals. He left each institution feeling they had not respected him enough. The misery of his career having been reset in the West was a scar that kept itching him. Beneath his veneer of accomplishment and happiness, he never felt he was quite entrenched enough, or appreciated enough, no matter how much he kept demonstrating his worth.

In his fifties he got kidney disease for the second time. He'd undergone a transplant in his late twenties, but now the kidney his sister Samira had gifted him had reached its expiration. Until a new kidney could be found for him, he needed daily dialysis. His approach was to hide this predicament from everyone at his work. I can't fully explain why, except to say that this is what feeling precarious means. It means you feel you cannot be a whole person, with vulnerabilities and needs, because it feels too risky. So Dr. Teebi drove to work at the Montreal Children's Hospital each morning as if nothing was the matter. At lunchtime, he drove back home, undressed to his undershirt, and hooked his body up to the dialysis machine so it could exchange his fluids, a process of draining and reinjection. An hour later, when the dialysis was over, he drove back to work to see more patients in the afternoon. In the evenings, once again at home, he collapsed from fatigue.

He kept this routine up for over a year, often lugging his dialysis setup with him on work trips or conferences. When a matching kidney was finally found, he had to take time off for the operation. His colleagues were astonished to hear he had been sick at all.

The vanishing of life assets that came with our displacement also made my father different with money. In our new life in the West, he grew much stingier, much more aware of money than he had ever been before. The hypercapitalism of his new society was no doubt a spur. As soon as he made money he'd invest it, scattering his investments in every country he had more than a passing familiarity with, as if trying to immunize our family against some chance upheaval rendering us penniless again. This behaviour persisted even after we had become comfortable again, even after he had housed and educated all his children. In what became his final years, my father returned to the Middle East to work—alone, without even my mother—because it paid more.

Like my father, my early time in America was also consumed with rebuilding. For me this meant trying to retrieve what I loved most about my prior life. My cousin Abed's family had been expelled from Kuwait after the war ended. They eventually landed in Germany, a place where none of them had connections or knew the language.

Abed and I wrote letters to each other. They took what seemed like months to travel between our new countries. In them we wrote about ways the partnership we started in Kuwait could stay alive—how we could continue our schemes and plans. We theorized that, actually, this dislocation was positive. We could go international now: I can helm the American branch of our company, and him the German branch.

Once a year or so, if our parents were feeling flush, they'd tell me and Abed to talk to each other on the phone for a minute or two, the long-distance charges be damned.

It was hard to keep this up. Each of us had more immediate problems. I had a whole culture to absorb: strange codes of conduct with schoolmates, new slang, ambiguous paths to being accepted—things a child absorbs osmotically from the time they're a baby, but which I had to figure out as a teenager. I'm sure the culture shock my cousin experienced in Germany was worse. In our letters, we may have been trying to pick up where we left off, but actually we were now much further back than before. There were many steps to retrace.

I was not conscious of this at the time, but it showed in my growing disinclination to keep connected to my faraway cousin. Our correspondence dwindled, and eventually stopped. Every one of our schemes died.

I did not reach out to or hear from Abed for many years.

In the early 2000s, Al Jazeera contacted my father asking if they could do a profile on him. Their Arabic satellite station ran a popular program highlighting stars of the Arab diaspora. They thought that Dr. Teebi, with his long list of scientific discoveries and accomplishments, would make for an interesting episode. My father, delighted by this recognition, quickly agreed.

In preparation for the arrival of the camera crew, the producer called him to discuss. There would be a long interview about his work, of course, but they also wanted other things. Could they film one of his classes of graduate students at the university? Was it possible to explore his family and daily life? Does he have any hobbies or interests to give colour?

The camera crew timed its visit for a weekend where there was a Muslim community picnic at a park in Mississauga. Our whole family went. We were instructed to walk around as a unit, pretending to converse as we were filmed. I led a kind of mocking meta-talk with my siblings, which my father predictably shushed. He treated the task with great seriousness. He gestured with his hands and spoke filler words to my mother—*Yes, as I told you, that's how it is, indeed, that's exactly right*—as we trudged between the trees while a cameraman backpedaled ahead of us with his rig.

They conducted a series of sit-down interviews with my father. The more professionally oriented discussions were in his office, where he spoke about the Arab genetic disorders that were his specialty. The more personal ones took place in more whimsical locations. One of them was filmed on a boat floating in a pond at the park. My father talked about his life as a migrant, the years of arduous rebuilding. It was affecting to hear his (and our) life summarized this way, a moment of reflection that he (and we) rarely had.

At some point, knowing the backstage machinations, it became obvious to me that my father had told Al Jazeera that he moonlighted as a poet. As part of his answer to what turned out to be the final segment of the program they aired, he looked at the camera and recited a poem.

My father was in his fifties at the time. He had gone

through many vicissitudes—success, failures, and wild fluctuations in circumstance. Yet the poem he chose to recite was one he wrote when he was a young man studying in Egypt. It was a poem about losing your sense of self in displacement. With their nod at the uncontrollable fleetness of time, the last lines of this poem are particularly haunting:

إن عمري قد يقارب ربع قرن،
دون ما ألقى هوية

My age approaches a quarter-century
And I have not found an identity

It was clear that my father felt a poem like this applied to his life in its winter as much as it had in its spring. The old pains still seared him, and had been reopened with our more recent displacement. Reading the poem myself, I felt the same.

But it seems to me that my father reached for that poem for an even sadder reason. The plain fact was that, since that early time of his life, he had not written much other poetry at all. He continued to think of himself as a poet. We as his family thought of him that way. He even said he was a poet to a TV production crew. But I don't recall any poems after Kuwait at all, save for a couple on the occasions of my sisters' weddings. Of all the inheritance he left us, poetry was what I looked for most in his things, and that's what I did not find.

But I understand. There was no time for that sort of thing. In his second exile, my father could not afford poems. His life was compressed into only what was most necessary for him and us.

I think back now on the poems of his youth, the ones that surprised me with their vigor and abandon. The ones that felt far-fetched and mythological. I think now that these verses may have been vows he made. My father was saying—to himself—that he would not let the memory of where he came from escape, that he would not let himself feel defeated like his father Said had felt. I see those poems now as motivational pieces for the decades my father still had ahead of him in a Palestinian body.

Even for me, reading them in the midst of a genocide, the sheer wilful aliveness of them felt like a raft in the storm waters of horror.

For humans there is a notion of permanence to every long-standing condition. It is a mythology that we choose to submit to, in the same way we submit to forces like colonialism or imperialism or anything else that governs us. The mythologies overwhelm us to such an extent that they seem inevitable and irreversible.

My father created his own counter-mythologies. I only mourn that he stopped.

– 3 –

Clarity and Blur

I have become, through the raising of children, an excellent lecturer. I've developed a versatile style: part classical didacticism grounded in individual choice and values, and part skeptical introspection and self-abasing humour. My greatest success is that my nineteen-year-old son does not roll his eyes too much.

By the end of the summer of 2024, as my son was getting ready for his first year of university, I wanted to talk to him about the treacherous road ahead. Not about navigating his workload or making friends. I wanted to talk to him about something far more basic: how to even speak.

By then, Israel's assault on Gaza had reached a point that was intolerable for most everyone in the world other than committed Zionists. It was not surprising that students everywhere, from Columbia University to the University of Toronto to the Free University of Berlin, took action. They'd watched in real time on their smartphones the workings of the colonial despotism that dominated their assigned readings—why wouldn't they try to rebel against such sordid soon-to-be histories? But one by one, the universities quelled the students. Some did it with instantaneous police violence, as if such a response was so obvious that it wasn't worth taking a moment to consider. Others indulged the students with charades of negotiations that often failed to produce even token divestiture. Yet others, like the University of Toronto, near where I live, used a court proceeding as a key tool. The court's decision, effusive in its love for the students speaking their principles, nonetheless produced the desired outcome, finding in property rights formalism grist enough to order their expulsion.

I visited some of the encampments before they were taken down. Reading about them from afar, what had first compelled me was not the sense that they could somehow stop the horrors, but that the students had simply insisted on at least being heard. When I read their statements and social media posts, I saw they had developed a clarity in stating their grievances, and what solutions they meant to extract. Their words seemed unencumbered by concerns of power, money, or class. I wanted to show them support, yes, but a selfish part of me also wanted to listen to how they talked. For my son's sake, I wanted to learn.

My first such visit sticks with me. Around this particular encampment the students had built a wire fence fortified with cardboard. Would-be visitors lined up to enter through a gate guarded by several students, the opening narrow enough that I could only slip through it sideways. Once I was let in, there was a kind of makeshift orientation desk, behind which was an exhausted-looking white student stealing bites from his falafel sandwich as he spoke to each visitor. He directed me to a handwritten sign listing the encampment's values—nondiscrimination, nonviolence, and the like. He then asked me some questions (why was I there? What did I intend to do?) and gave me instructions (don't go in the tents, don't photograph faces, respect the space).

Once inside, what I saw stunned me. Here, in a city in North America, I saw students of all ethnicities and backgrounds sitting in public with Palestinian flags and slogans all around them. The details were the thing. Each of the tents in the encampment was named either after a neighbourhood in Gaza, newly famous for its hemorrhaging wounds, or after a city in historical Palestine, some famous like my own hometown of Jaffa, and some quite obscure. The students had graffitied in various places quotes from Mahmoud Darwish, from Norman Finkelstein, from the Quran, representing all creeds. There was a small library, with bean bags for readers. Some students had a keffiyeh wrapped around their faces—from their eyes and eyebrows, I could tell many were Arab or Black. Other students kept their faces uncovered, whether due to privilege, daring, or something else.

For an identity long relegated to the shadows, the love and overtness with which these students supported Palestine crushed me. They were behaving as more than just emblems of the sociopolitical structures into which they were born, but as human beings with empathy for other human beings, however remote from them geographically and otherwise. I walked around quiet as a ferret, too astonished to socialize with anyone.

At some point I noticed that the student who interviewed me at the gate was following me, monitoring from a distance. He seemed both suspicious of me, but also afraid to approach. Instead of waiting, I walked over to him: Is there something wrong? He said that I'd been taking lots of pictures, and the encampment had already had incidents of threats and confrontations with outside individuals and groups. I showed him the photo roll on my phone. I said: See? No faces. I only wanted to show some of the tents to my family's group chat. He sighed in relief and touched me on the shoulder. It was like he could finally talk.

Where I had admired the encampments for their clarity, this student, like most others I spoke to, said they felt neither heard nor understood. They often went in circles with the administration, which pounded away at unrelated concerns meant to quiet the students rather than respond to them. Meanwhile, everywhere in the media the students were vilified, their plain and unmistakable language seemingly the main source of the outrage. Much of that language had grown out of slogans of Palestinian resistance for seventy-plus years: "Free Palestine," "From the River to the Sea," "End the Occupation." For that, they were labeled by the mainstream media as inflammatory, even threatening. Their removal became a matter of crazed urgency, monitored for developments on an hourly basis. The students were branded—by lobby groups who were then quoted and parroted in newspapers and on TV—as antisemites, as terror supporters, even as genocidal themselves. Most times during the day, there were now counter-protestors parked around the perimeter of the encampment, armed with zoom cameras and well-studied instigation tactics, ready to harass the students and any supporters visiting them.

The clarity that I'd admired about the students was what was deemed most threatening. The fluency of the encampments was their violence.

I realized, fairly quickly, that far from helping me figure out what to tell my son, my visits to the encampments only complicated my sense of what was permissible. The confusion reminded me of feelings I had before, in my own university days.

When I was eighteen I tried my hand at writing something about Palestine for the first time. It was an article for the student newspaper of my CEGEP, part of the Quebec collegiate system that precedes university. I don't recall its specifics, but in the subsequent issue of the newspaper, a much longer article appeared as a response to mine. I will never forget the headline: "A Rose by Any Other Name." The thrust of the article was that while I may be entitled to my wrongful opinion about the Middle East, what I must not be permitted to do is refer to a "Palestine" in any serious context. A "Palestine" was not a place that existed, was not recognized internationally by any state of consequence, and using the word constitutes an enormous injury to Jews everywhere. The newspaper had been wrong to even publish me.

This incident wasn't special: it's an experience so commonplace for Palestinians in exile that it induces not outrage but eye rolls. What strikes me about it now is that I can't remember the contents of my own article. That piece was the first time I wrote about my homeland. In the five years that had by then elapsed since my family's arrival in North America, I had resolved to abandon our omnipresent state of fear about our identity. Despite this new environment that seemed hostile to us in much franker ways than I had experienced in the Middle East, I wanted to be bold, unreserved. This article was my first foray in that direction. I'm sure it offered no groundbreaking opinion or insight, but shouldn't I recall something about it? I don't. At most I can try to triangulate possibilities according to the epoch and my preoccupations at that time. What I do remember well is the response, the one that told me: Sit down, boy, you don't know how to behave among us here.

I was too young to be much burdened by this experience. I felt sure that I had invited the backlash by some defect or other in my still-developing linguistic capabilities. If I fixed these defects—which I was madly driven to—I'd be home free.

I have an abiding faith in language. I trace it to a hereditary fascination with Arabic poetry, which always felt to me like a special kind of music, steeped in rhythm, metre, and wit. My father, like many Arabs of a certain era, preferred Ahmad Shawqi or Ibrahim Tuqan. I used to catch him doodling calligraphy of their verses on the back of Kleenex boxes as he talked to someone on the phone. I also remember my two grandfathers—Said and Shaban— across from each other at a backgammon table, chattering between rolls of the dice and glides of the checkers. As their game wore on, sometimes a subtle argument— about politics, or suspicions of cheating—might pool between them. One of them would seek a decisive blow by reciting from memory a choice verse. A favourite was the poet Antarah ibn Shaddad, the ancient knight of Jahiliyyah, son of a warrior and an enslaved Black woman from Ethiopia. The selection would be so pointed and deadly that I expected its recipient to immediately raise a white flag in submission. Except that in short order the other grandfather would thunder back, marshaling for his counterattack verses from Abu Nuwas or Al-Mutanabbi. They would keep trading lines, their barbs for each other implied in the verses they'd chosen to recite. At some point, their argument no longer mattered. Their enjoyment of the words won over the polemic, and they clapped each other on the shoulder and went on playing.

It wasn't always like that: sometimes the accusations of subterfuge did not dissipate, and sometimes the backgammon board was thrown; my grandfathers' table was not Geneva. Still, I sensed in their linguistic spars a seemingly limitless power to confront and conciliate.

That was the limitlessness I sought when I entered McGill University. Ostensibly I was there to begin the journey of becoming a doctor like my father. But in my heart I considered that a side mission that must be checked off so I could experience all the other things I craved. Most of all the freedom to think and say and do whatever I wished, far from paternal oversight.

I found the Muslims first. I had an observant upbringing, for a time going with my family to the mosque multiple evenings a week to congregate with others in the community, before I drifted away in my late teens. But at McGill the sense of communal safety of being among Muslims did not exist; I saw instead how we had to operate in the margins. We had conceived of ourselves not as central actors in the school, but as bit players being kindly accommodated. There was a timidity in us, a willingness to accept whatever someone in authority told us, and a disinclination to even ask for what we wanted. We had a Friday prayer hall to which thousands of students and faculty flocked every week; if at the last minute we were told it had to be taken over by another group for some function, we just accepted it and canceled the prayer, or directed people to pray outside on the lawn. One of our graduate student leaders—who was about thirty-five, the sort of age that seems ancient to a freshman—advised us not to rock the boat, or risk our privileges being taken away altogether. I remember thinking: I'm not looking for any more fathers, thank you.

Within a year of my arrival I was leading the Muslim association. But even in leadership, I felt like an edge figure, a person prone to bluster and aggressiveness that were not justified by his modest levels of piety. I organized a couple of protests in support of Palestine—only five or six people attended each one, from our association of thousands. My projects stalled between the hyper-caution that ruled everyone's approach and the growing disinterest that overtook mine.

My desire for confrontation led me to the debate team that met in the basement of the Shatner student building. Unlike my Muslim friends, these people seemed to have never had a moment of timidity in their lives. They were almost uniformly white, and forever drunk both on liquor and an excess of their own self-assurance. They were willing to argue the wildest of ideas, always steeped in a political and cultural soil that I'd never walked. When they erupted in laughter at jokes about Hegel and Nietzsche, it was like a foreign dialect to someone like me who'd been herded to the sciences. I was jealous of their knowledge, their abandon. Once or twice I tried to even the playing field by proposing for debate some resolution about Palestine and Israel. The first time I did that the room went quiet for a moment, before someone snickered and said, "Of all places, this is not where you want to argue about this sort of thing," to guffaws from all those around. That was the end of it, even though I was mystified at what he may have meant.

The feeling repeated itself often. So many of my conversations with these people, and at university in general, felt like they were blind steps toward an inevitable trip-wire whose existence I only discovered after it was too late. I suppose even the clearest signs were not clear to me back then. I remember on several occasions members of the debating team referring with reverence to their association with the likes of Irwin Cotler, a politician, lawyer, and hardened Israeli activist who was on the faculty at McGill.

I was stuck on the edges of two groups: people who had things to communicate but were afraid to, and people united by their love for communication but who refused to communicate with me.

Mostly I educated myself, in private. Communities can only nurture those who feel a part of them, and I felt a part of none. Every piece of learning I gained demonstrated to me how much more I was missing. My parents, in our forced exodus, had sheltered us from so much of Western culture that even normal doses of it felt overwhelming sometimes.

My greatest discovery came in the stacks of the McLennan Library. This is where I met a dilapidated copy of *Lolita*, out of place, tossed on the bottom rack of an empty metal shelf. I remember the moment the way you remember first love. I read each of the book's paragraphs two or three times, because of disbelief at their beauty, and also because I couldn't understand much of what I was reading. It took me many weeks to finish it, and months more for Vladimir Nabokov's other works. Along the way I filled many Hilroy notebooks with his words and their definitions, believing that if I absorbed his vocabulary I might absorb his mastery, too. I exhausted my siblings with demands that they quiz me on these notebooks that I memorized forward and back.

I found books and journal papers that annotated Nabokov, which did me the favour of decoding in footnotes all his obscure allusions. I scoured them to trace my new idol back to his idols. Soon Pushkin, Gogol, and Chekhov, among others, became mine too. They all had their charms, and turned into lifelong companions, although for me none surpassed Nabokov. It was perhaps a strange clique for a young Palestinian in Montreal, but it didn't feel that way to me. It was only with these writers that I felt limitless instead of liminal.

Looking back, I see that I was desperate for solutions to the problem of how to present myself. Nabokov was the first writer I encountered who institutionalized in his work a certain ambiguity, a disregard for being understood, which he emphasized with bemused trickery. I could not grasp everything in him, and on some level I suspected he was hiding what he wanted to say. I saw that as a positive. Form could be an obfuscator, an end unto itself. Clarity—in literature as in my new life—could be optional. As someone whose attempts at clarity had been thwarted, and who was beginning to see the advantages of hiding, it was a relief.

The exile in me also loved him. Nabokov had been forced to leave his hometown of St. Petersburg due to the Russian Revolution, but in many of his fictions that exile seemed an incidental matter, almost a trifle. His characters, down to their very psyches, felt like they'd been created in defiance of time and place. For Nabokov this originated in a philosophy that elevated his aesthetics above everything else, including his societal context, its politics and traumas. But for me the attraction was rooted in something less principled: a desire to *escape* my identity, and the problems that identity posed. Not even a year into university, I now worried about who I was talking to, what I could say to them, and how. My obsession with my audience—an audience that I never much had, or figured to have—was near total. How could I present concepts, like my very Palestinianness, that were not palatable? It felt like a gift to find a writer who seemed to say that you don't even have to try.

If Nabokov was my personal patron saint, Leonard Cohen was all of Montreal's, and McGill especially. He, too, demonstrated to me the attractiveness of inscrutability. Cohen seemed to have an ability to express forbidden things, about women, religion, politics. Was that a whiff of Jewish supremacy that I detected in one of his songs? I wondered. That he sometimes left me mystified made him more appealing. Perhaps being *confusing* was the key to being accepted, I thought. I've never had a poster of any person on my walls, except for Leonard Cohen. I bought a five-by-seven-inch black-and-white framed portrait of him from a street seller and hung it above my desk.

For a while I pretended to be a poet. I latched onto a poetry group that hung out together to critique our scribbles. I remember once writing a poem about the Oslo Accords—who hasn't?—and submitting it for discussion. When it was my turn, the faculty advisor, a Kennedyesque man in looks and attempted diplomacy, convened the workshop by saying that we should be careful to not engage with the political elements of this piece, and focus on poetics and such instead.

I read hardly any Arab or Muslim writers at McGill. I was too much in thrall with English to take what I was afraid would be a backward look like that. I did find Emile Habibi in the stacks, and Jabra Ibrahim Jabra, and Ahdaf Soueif. But I found myself in need of more context for them than my father had given me, or that I could source on my own. I sampled Edward Said—he provided context, but I could not afford to spare much of my ESL-paced reading on his work, which did not offer me the escape of the fictions I preferred. I did see him speak at McGill once. I recall an overflowing hall, and a barrage of harassing questions. He stood at the podium, gaunt in his cheeks, valiant but harried, trying to defend a one-state solution. I felt sadness for him, and pity.

My father had long derided my affinity for jidal— useless argument—and I could almost see why now.

Everywhere I looked at McGill, I could not find for myself a mirror that reflected what I wanted to see. I had been delighted to escape my father's prisons, but now that I was free, I realized plenty of people had built more elaborate prisons for me. I could not find a way to speak or write, in this state of exile, as a Palestinian. It was like I had to invent something novel just to exist.

— — —

The controls on Palestinians' use of language have always been severe, so much that we have gotten used to silencing ourselves before others do it for us.

Especially early on in the genocide, in October or November 2023, Palestinians were rarely called to appear on TV or radio programs to discuss the events in Gaza. But even when invited, some of us hesitated to accept, or outright refused. The tripwire that I felt in my university years still existed, and the context was now far more inflamed. We were afraid of saying the wrong thing in the heat of a live argument (for there is always an argument). We couldn't even determine what may be construed as the wrong thing. People worried about how they would be edited by news programs or stripped of context. Many would not subject themselves to the indignity of being required to disclaim an allegiance to Hamas as the price of entry into a conversation. After the millions of reports and pictures of Palestinians mutilated and dead seemed to not move anyone to action, we could not trust that language would do us justice. If our flesh didn't move you, why would our words?

This disconnect exists because the main language through which the West understands Palestinians is that of terrorism. I could see it in the very first linguistic act of the military campaign on Gaza: its branding. In the wake of the October 7 incursions, Israel's attacks on Gaza instantaneously became known as the "Israel-Hamas war." That was the verbiage the Israeli government used, and it was picked up whole by every mainstream outlet. At first it could seem like an act of care and specificity, one that indicated Israel's quarrel was not with all Palestinians, but only with one group. That is a thin veneer. The effect of the branding was to hide that those actually affected by the attacks were Palestinians (regardless of political affiliation), while at the same time paradoxically implying that any Palestinians killed by Israel belonged to Hamas. If Al-Qaeda had attacked America and called it a war on the Republican Party, no one would have accepted it, and yet branding in a similar vein became standard in the Gaza war.

The handiness of calling it "the Israel-Hamas war" is that it is not just a name, but a ruling. It tells you all you need to know about which side is good and which evil. If Hamas is a terror organization, which the political apparatuses in the West have long deemed it to be, then whatever feelings you have about Israel, it is the only side to which you may give your sympathy and support. In fact, Israel is the only side that you will not be subject to criminal penalties for supporting. The language itself becomes a way of boxing you into a political position out of which there is no viable escape.

Such is the power of the word "terrorist"—never mind that, as many have noted, there may not be a vaguer term in the world. However it's defined in *Oxford* or *Merriam-Webster*, the practical connotations of the word are of Arabs or Muslims acting with barbarity against Western liberal values. You most easily perceive these connotations when, every once in a while, some news organization gestures at even handedness by describing as terrorists people who do not fit the habitual image. In those cases they have to add qualifiers: white nationalist terrorists, or Russian terrorists, et cetera. In its original flavour, "terrorist" does not require qualifiers of "Arab" or "Muslim"; these identities are assumed until further notice. Try it out: "Arab terrorists" sounds mealymouthed or redundant to an ear trained in the West.

The blurriness of the word is key to its power to erase context. Among the sub-projects of contemporary Zionism, decontextualization of Palestinian resistance is a high priority. Once someone has been branded a terrorist, further information about them is unnecessary, even offensive, unless it further corroborates the branding. The terrorist kills, abducts, rapes, and beheads children. The reason you believe they do this is because they are terrorists, and they are terrorists because they do it; the circularity of the logic somehow confirms it. The word "terrorist" is a magical container of pure inhumanity—ahistorical, unspecific, but unquestioned. The branding is a prophylactic against anyone attempting to puncture it with measly tools like facts or evidence. Israel branded respected nonprofit organizations as terror supporters, and somehow that became sufficient to discredit these organizations' painstaking findings about Israel. The West followed that lead, expanding to new targets. When students at Toronto's Lincoln Alexander School of Law attempted in a statement to provide historical context for Hamas's attacks on Israel, legal practitioners throughout Canada rushed to condemn the students and add their names to a hiring blacklist. Their crime was that they used the language of facts and nuance when such tools were not permissible in regards to people pre-branded as terrorists.

The otherness of the terrorist's conduct is, to us reasonable and peaceable humans, absolute. The distance it creates is critical to their dehumanization, to the discounting of their history and goals. We consider cows to be distant from our species, and so most believe they may be slaughtered as needed. Terrorists, similarly distant from us, can be sent to slaughter too, them and their children.

The distancing—born in language, not observed reality—is never applied with symmetry. Israel, never called "terrorist" in mainstream outlets, has every opportunity to contextualize the horrific acts it commits. When the US Congress welcomes a foreign head of state, and rewards his speechmaking with record numbers of ovations, it is obvious that such a state's language is privileged, its context relevant, its actions rooted in wants and needs that are reasonable and justifiable.

CLARITY AND BLUR

Free from the application of terms like "terrorist," persons and entities committing crimes against humanity are able to continue thinking of, and presenting, themselves in human terms. At the end of 2023, when Israel's conduct was becoming so flagrant that South Africa brought a case for genocide at the International Court of Justice, several intellectuals on the so-called Israeli left began having public conversations (frequently in English) about Israel's offensive in Gaza being a war "for the soul of Israel." It was familiar language—recycled from discourses on previous offensives, annexations, and apartheid actions. The language is designed to elicit empathy, because it implies some kind of thoughtful, tortured wrestling with the violence Israel undertakes.

But the reason this posturing was possible at all was because Israeli humanness was never in question. Absent the branding of terrorism, Israel's crimes against humanity escaped being considered, in the official record, as anathema to our very values as human beings. Rather, they were a matter Israel could be said to have wrestled with in its very soul—even if most every wrestling match Israel has ever had with its soul seems to end with Palestinians getting pinned.

A human is a creature of roiling desires. You see it from the time a person is born wailing for food to the time they are near death and desperate for another breath. Desire is rooted in imagining that something might improve our lives. But desire without a baseline of expression dies. If you cannot speak what you desire, how long can it stay desired inside you before it withers away into oblivion?

When I call for Palestine to be free "from the river to the sea," it is not a mere slogan, it is a demand that is deeply personal. My family is from Jaffa and its environs, which via violent colonization and dispossession came to be located in modern-day Israel. Palestinians, whether they come from the West Bank, Gaza, or from exile like me, are barred from going to live in that area. Any Jewish person anywhere in the world may come to live in the land of my ancestors, but I cannot. It is an unfairness so intense that it sears me to think about it. For me, the right of return—specifically the return *there*, to Jaffa, that specific plot—is as personal a right as there exists in the Palestinian cause. I've imagined it so many times I feel almost pathetic. And Jaffa is only my particular cynosure. Other exiled Palestinians dream of ancestral towns and villages everywhere in pre-1948 Palestine, which stretched from the Jordan River to the Mediterranean Sea. When we mention those bodies of water, we are telling you what we want for ourselves and our future.

But I acknowledge that is not the sole meaning. For some Palestinians, the phrase means their desire to have the freedom to move across areas where they are barred or impeded. For yet others it means sovereignty, for others the freedom to create an entirely new system of governance of that land. Ultimately, when Palestinians say "from the river to the sea," they are asserting their belonging to a land in which their increasing disappearance is a societal and governmental mandate. That there is a multiplicity of specific desires encoded in those words reflects the heterogeneous nature of humanity.

When language is made forbidden, the real aim of it is to silence our desires. It is the best way to dehumanize us, to render us into animals caged in a corner, observed but not listened to. The would-be master's first move is always to strip away humanity. No tool is fitter for that purpose than taking away language.

I understand that language feels more dangerous in the shorter forms of slogans and social media posts. By comparison, what I write here lives in a sconce of relative (but *only* relative) safety because it has the advantage of length and nuance. Maybe this makes it more dismissible. I am unlikely to capture an imagination or foment a revolution. The shorter forms are the ones that are more readily grasped and activate masses of people. Simple, normative phrases like "Free Palestine" cause some to worry. For me, "Free Palestine" describes, with good precision, what is desired: freedom for a place called Palestine, the name of the land given to it by its inhabitants—the Palestinians—since before the Middle Ages. To those who colonized that land, the danger of such frank expression of Palestinian desire must seem overwhelming. And so they cast suspicion on the precision of the language. They impute it with ill intent. The *only* way Palestine can be free, they claim, is if the Jews are exterminated. The language is, in this light, rendered disingenuous and blurry. The absurdity of the interpretation is beside the point.

I have often felt language to be unfit for describing what Israel perpetrated on Gaza. I don't mean that language couldn't describe it, I meant that the descriptions didn't matter in the same way they mattered in other contexts. If we read a news report about a massacre committed on the streets of Chicago, for example, we'd gasp and buckle. We'd talk about it for years after it happened, wince at the thought of it, and fixate on how we could have prevented it. And yet when Palestinians became subject to a fresh massacre every day, our response was to become inured to the word itself. I have wondered if the word "massacre" had become defective, if there were a repair shop to which I could send it to be looked over and fixed. But it wasn't just one word. Language itself lost its main power, communication. It lost its ability to awaken and alarm or elicit sympathy.

A month or two into the assault on Gaza, the word "genocide" began to be used. At first I shied away from it (a sort of hoping against hope that it wouldn't be true), but I understood the readiness of some to use it. After awful terms like "massacres" had made no impression on Western powerbrokers, no doubt some hoped that by associating what was happening with a kind of third rail of evil, they'd be able to generate enough alarm to stop the killings. But even as Israel carpet-bombed Gaza, media and governments repeatedly advised us that no one should use a term like "genocide" absent a doctorate in international law. It is a serious legal term with serious legal requirements. Using it to describe Israeli conduct, we were told, would be grossly unfair and dangerous to Israel, a mark of a reckless propagandist. I'd not before encountered such insistent objections to colloquial uses of other legal terms, like murder, trespass, hate crime, or even genocide if perpetrated by other regimes—but in the case of cruelties perpetrated upon Palestinians, things are always different. Rather than describing the massacres of our people, we were reduced to haggling over whether our vocabulary is too harsh on those committing the massacres.

We betray language itself by allowing the oppressor to destroy its communicative core in service of domination and protecting the status quo. We betray language when we let it be what primes the body for the violence that its oppressors have planned for it. The students of the encampments were branded as violent and dangerous because of their speech; this was a necessary prelude to enacting the actual violence of destroying the encampments and imprisoning or deporting the protestors. A US congresswoman of Palestinian descent used the term "from the river to the sea," but was censured by her colleagues—a putatively powerful individual shunned by a much more powerful institution. The head of a social media platform called the same phrase a "euphemism" that must "necessarily imply genocide." Despite avowing free speech absolutism, he committed to removing all instances of the phrase on his platform.

In the face of actual violence waged against them, Palestinians are tried and convicted of presumptive violence for their language. Our words are assumed to be code words or dog whistles that mean something else, necessarily more nefarious than what we say they mean. The result is that we are barred from the language that everyone else uses. We are made to cram into a different, much more limited and inexact language, one that is unfit for what we want to express, but proximate to the danger we supposedly present. The usual language remains available to the rest of the world to use freely. It is only Palestinians and their allies who have been segregated out of it, a linguistic apartheid that applies to us wherever we are in the same way that the geographic apartheid applies to us in occupied Palestine.

In the end, we, and what we want, are forever pushed out, even in language. It reminds me of some lines from Darwish, who was never a stranger to quashed desires:

CLARITY AND BLUR

لم يَبْقَ في اللغة الحديثةِ هامشٌ
للإجتفاءِ بما نحبُّ
فكلُّ ما سيكونُ . . . كانْ

There is no margin left in modern language
to celebrate what we love
So all that will be . . . was

The sinister blurriness ascribed to Palestinians is mirrored, as if in a dark river, by the privilege of blurriness
that Zionists reserve for themselves. When I name my
oppressors, both historically and in the present moment,
I have used the word "Zionist." I mean it as its founders
meant it: a political ideology of colonizing Palestine for
Jewish people. It was clear to these early Zionists that
they had to take land that did not belong to them from
people who would resist them fiercely. They wrote of it
extensively in their publications and correspondence and
diaries from that time. The same ideology underpins how
Israel perpetuates and grows itself today, extracting ever
more land and getting rid of ever more Palestinians.

Nonetheless, my ability to use the word "Zionist" is now
threatened. Those bastions of thought and expression, the
universities, have become, through the work of their administrators in the post-encampment world, the starting

point for this project. In Harvard or New York University, for example, one is now not permitted to besmirch "Zionists," as these universities have now codified protections for the word in their policies. When I say "Zionist," NYU now assumes I'm using it as a hate speech code word, hiding a hatred of Jews in the guise of denouncing ideology. That the blurring of "Jew" and "Zionist" has been rejected by many Jews (and, no less importantly, by me too) is immaterial. In NYU's view, what I really have in my heart is hatred, but I use different words in a canny attempt to avoid ostracization. The circumscription of language is a way to strip us of our own hearts. What's in us does not belong to us, because it has already been revealed to be vile by NYU.

The victim, in this conception, is the one who must always be very careful not to offend the oppressor, but the oppressor is so blurred as to be almost impossible to capture in words. The blur leads to uncertainty, the uncertainty leads to fear, and the fear leads to the ultimate intended consequence: silence. The policing of language makes it so that what we say is no longer important; what's important is to say it in conformance with the standards of those whose first preference is that we don't say it at all. Trying to speak as a Palestinian is a state of being besieged by the very tools you need to break the siege.

Even if I considered the use of "Zionism" to be a gray area for potential hate speech—which it is not—erring on the side of banning the gray areas results in hampering speech altogether. Free speech should not need me to advocate for it. It is a core right, even if it is often bandied about by odious people seeking to be allowed their odiousness.

To be sure, however, my thoughts and desires as a Palestinian are not odious. I don't want people to let me speak because I am an edge case for which Voltaire runs to mount a heroic defence. I am not that, at all. No, I should speak because I am the core of what Voltaire claimed to stand for—an appeal to reason for the sake of human progress.

It is tempting to think that there is one moment that crystallizes to a person what they must do, the life choice they must make. A moment of clarity that makes everything click, that makes them change their course.

But during my time at McGill, there was no specific moment when I determined to stop presenting myself as Palestinian. It didn't take some major clapback to silence me, some definite transgression that I committed and for which I was punished. I certainly did not need a media firestorm at some encampment to let me know.

I was too sensitive to my surroundings to need that. Instead, I came to see all the small reactions I got from people: the shrinking body language, slight repulsions, bit lips, awkward smiles, hesitations, changes of subject, veiled jokes, evaporated connections—the accumulation of dozens of little cues and clues. With every new indication, I inched further toward caution about myself, about stating who I was. Eventually, I understood beyond doubt that my identity was unwanted.

I learned that I cannot use language as a set of agreed-upon definitions, or rules of construction that I could use to express myself. I re-understood it as a set of rules that were available to others. There was nothing in this society that seemed like it could accommodate me, nor did I feel I could defy it. Nabokov, for example, rebelled against the common parlance in his unconforming linguistic constructions and word usage, shibboleths of his foreigner status. But the common parlance for me, unlike it was for him, wasn't just a matter of aesthetics. It contained the key to acceptance or rejection, both of myself and my ideas. I found I was not strong enough to insist on my own parlance, and had no community to rely on to legitimize or grow it. I was alone in a language I longed to find community in.

I am ashamed I was not strong enough to insist like the students at the encampments did. The truth is I cared what others thought. I so wished to be accepted that I cared *a lot*.

I stopped outwardly identifying as a Palestinian. I stopped bringing it up in conversation. I became "Mediterranean," or, if someone pressed me on the matter, even a miscellaneous Arab. Whatever language I could find to blur myself away, I used. My light skin was convenient for cloaking.

The uncertainty I had about myself interfered with every aspect of my life, including my studies. Compared to the challenge of trying to understand myself and interact with other humans, my premed program seemed wretched and unmeaningful. I had no interest in finding out about the processes of human cells, or all their hormones and enzymes. I was not comfortable with the exterior of my body, so what did I care about its innards? My attention, never a strong suit, sagged to nothingness. Soon I was skipping more classes than I attended, and sometimes I skipped exams too if taking them felt like an exercise in futility. Before long, McGill kicked me out. My GPA over my first two years had become untenable.

I felt like a monumental failure. I had never experienced anything like that before in my life. It was embarrassing enough that I hid it from everyone, including my family. By then I had gotten the hang of pretending to be someone I wasn't, so more hiding wasn't difficult.

Deep down, I did not think of my academic failure as a total loss. In the back of my mind, I had decided to write anyway. Liberated from the burden of classes, I wrote every day, working from an apartment on Aylmer Street in the so-called McGill Ghetto. I focused on form because I was afraid of substance. I wrote long, flowery descriptions of park pigeons. I wrote paragraphs replete with devices and metaphors that were about themselves rather than their ostensible subjects. I compared, page for page, my paragraphs with those of my idols.

I knew something was missing. I never submitted anything I wrote.

A few years after I was out of university, I was working as a programmer. I had no training to speak of in computer science. It was a job I fell into, and it snowballed into a career. I did no more work than I needed to, and spent the rest of the day writing what I told myself would one day be a novel.

Here and there I attended creative writing workshops at a local college. The contrived pieces that I submitted impressed no one. The instructor had kind words, as instructors tend to, but hardly affirmation.

Toward the end of the course the instructor announced a short fiction contest for creative writing students. The prize was a monetary award and publication in a journal. In front of the class I asked a few questions about the contest requirements and rules, even though I had no piece anywhere near suitable for submission.

As everyone walked out of the classroom, I overheard two of my fellow students snickering about my questions, and my writing. They must have thought they were out of earshot, or didn't care if they were. I am a veteran at being slighted, but it never ceases to incense me.

The deadline was three weeks away. I told my then-wife I would win that award. I had no basis for believing that, but I wanted to put myself in trouble that I could only escape by succeeding. My son was still a baby at the time. I wrote every night after I put him to bed, with a kind of single-mindedness I never had before.

The result was a short story titled "Teresa." Set in Kuwait, it was about a Muslim family that hired a Filipino maid. To the ten-year-old son of this family, Teresa is an outré figure, both in her Christianity and her salaciousness, the latter of which is represented in the story by her writing letters to her boyfriend back in the Philippines. The young boy becomes jealous. When Teresa's boyfriend eventually arrives in Kuwait to take a role as a foreign worker himself, the boy tries to obstruct his reunion with Teresa. The story ends with a horrible revelation.

I submitted the story to the contest, my first time submitting anything. A few months later, I was notified by a phone call that I'd won.

After an initial period of pride and vindication, my feelings about this "winning" story changed. I considered all the ways my narrative could have been attractive to the panel that had adjudicated the contest. In the story, the Muslim family views the Christian maid as an interloper. The family brandishes all the power they have over the maid—money, residence, her passport that they keep. They repudiate in the maid values that a Western society would consider normal, namely the boyfriend-girlfriend relationship. Critically, the boy in the family exhibits at a young age a sexual appetite that terrorizes and consumes the vulnerable maid. His barbarity had sprung so young that it is implied to be foundational.

The truth is that I'd not been conscious of all the tropes I had inserted in the story. But the narrative I concocted could scarcely have been more designed to curry favour with a white audience. What bothered me was not that I had portrayed my Arab and Muslim characters doing reprehensible things. It was that they did reprehensible things in precise confluence with the expectations of the society I now lived in.

I was conscious that I hadn't given the family in my story a specific ethnicity. I'd thought of them as Palestinian, but I never stated it. Part of me also did not want to associate the horribleness of this character—a character that was entirely a work of my imagination—with Palestinians. But mostly, I did not want to associate my name, as a person and a writer, with that identity.

The language I thought I had mastered had led me to an appalling narrative, a representation that I thought would be most acceptable in my world.

I remember meeting one of the judges at the prize ceremony. He gave me some anodyne advice: Keep writing.

Instead of heeding his words, I left writing entirely. I was sickened by myself. I sensed that my desire to succeed as a writer outweighed my principles, or my ability to recognize my principles.

I was not clear enough to write—about myself or anything. I needed to stop. For over a decade, I did.

– 4 –

Stories and Their Telling

In the summer of 1997, I felt large.

This was at the Allenby Bridge border crossing. My father and I were waiting to be let into Palestine, but there was no guarantee it would happen. On the other hand, I felt large. I felt larger and stronger than I ever thought I could be.

I got up to walk around. I searched for my reflection in the windows of that humid room. Look at those shoulders of mine. It's daytime and the windows were dusty, but you could tell.

By then we had moved from the US to Canada, where my father finally got his first permanent position in North America. In our living room back in Montreal, we had a glass cabinet. It was for our guest plates and my mother's crystal, but I used it to steal glances at myself now and then. Especially from a distance, when my father had corralled me to stand beside him for prayer. Though he always felt immense to me, in the reflection he is slumped, and his eyes are downcast. We are supposed to pray shoulder-to-shoulder, but his shoulders seemed far below mine. There was almost no contact.

I felt so large, to myself.

That Israeli soldier guarding the exit door at Allenby? Even in his boots and bulky uniform, he was not as large as me. I kept measuring him with my eyes. He had a sparse beard, and a long, black slab of armament dangling carelessly across him. He seemed to have a breathing problem because he kept holding two fingers against one nostril and blowing.

His wrists were thin. I'd been doing some boxing at the time, so I knew that was a disadvantage.

My father sat on a narrow bench against the wall. He rubbed his eyes with his palms. Not long ago, we had gotten our US citizenship, our first proper papers. He'd taken me on this trip for his own sake, really. I was his eldest, and he was running out of time with me. I had shown signs of being wayward. I'd already had a year at McGill, my halfway house to total freedom. I'd been making a point of talking in front of him about all the political events I took part in at school, knowing he wouldn't approve. Now he wanted to show me our homeland before it was too late. Despite—or maybe because of—our rocky relationship, he chose me as the first person in the family to take to Palestine.

He said: You'll see the land you like so much to argue about. You'll hear its stories.

We spent the week before in Amman. To my father, the potency of our new passports only went so far. So he called several acquaintances long-distance to strategize on what could be safely said to the border officers. He took notes, asked follow-ups. Can you give me the names and numbers of people who were *refused* entry? he asked. I'd like to call them to see what I should avoid.

Eventually, he came up with a speech that felt safe:

I am an American doctor living in Canada, and this is my son, a student. We'd like to visit for a week or so. To see Jerusalem, and maybe Jaffa if it's okay to cross. Just for tourism. I might give a lecture or two at Birzeit University, on the subject of genetics, since they invited me. I am a scientist, only a scientist.

Not one word, he warned me hours ago when we were standing in line, pressing his index finger against his lips. I will do all the talking, you don't say a word.

This sort of ban is old hat to me, it's uncontroversial. Even if my English has become fluid while his remains halting. Even if I feel I am getting good at forming an argument and communicating it. We are in a sensitive situation, and this is a sensitive subject. It is no spot for the young and foolish like me.

But my father's words did not work, even after five hours of waiting. My father repeated his speech to three different officers, each less impressed than the last. They'd disappear behind closed doors with our passports and rematerialize with questions. Who do you know in Jerusalem? And what is so special about Jaffa? What *else* are you lecturing about? Have you not heard me telling you to undress?

It was August, and boiling in that waiting room. My father's shirt showed three dark circles of sweat. He submitted another loud sigh, in the hopes that one of our aloof detainers would remember we were still there. None even noticed.

I looked out the window, past my reflection, at the terrain outside. The buff landscape was dotted with shags of pale green trees.

I remember thinking my father's words were too safe. They did not include any relevant arguments in our favour at all. They included no principle like *We are entitled to enter this land.* They did not include a truism like *Were it not for the violence of your forebears, we'd be the ones checking your passports, not vice versa.* They didn't even include mention of our relatives in Gaza—the living proof of our connection to the land—which my father purposely omitted to avoid opening up unnecessary stories and scrutiny. Instead, my father's words to these officers seemed mostly like . . . begging.

His words didn't work—but what if my largeness did?

The puny soldier by the exit could not take me. His vulgar weapon was only a small detail. His fellow soldiers and administrators everywhere inside and outside this crossing: equally small details. What match were they for my power, and my knowledge that I am right?

The thought of taking what's mine was intoxicating.

I was nineteen years old. I had brawn, a streak of recklessness, and the advantage of feeling, at long last, *this close* to home.

The greatest battleground in any war is always that of story. It is the heady spray of raison d'être that clears the path for strategy, whether the strategy is military, political, social, or economic. In my view, Israel's greatest accomplishment is that, even decades after its colonial inception, its story has remained in the foreground, while the stories of the Palestinian natives to the land continue to exist in relative obscurity.

Of course the obscurity of the Palestinian story is a manufactured one, a whole cloth tailored to fit snug over the minds of Western audiences. It takes forms too numerous to count, from the suppression of our news, however significant, beneath the seams of the front page, to the compacting of our bodies into bloodless statistics, to the amplification of the sins of the occupied and the expunging of the sins of the occupier, to the passive voice and other pet tools of the gatekeepers of narrative. All this is necessary because the Palestinian story is, in its very existence, a refutation of the founding Zionist mythology of a land without people.

Whenever it did trickle out of obscurity, the Palestinian story came with limits that mirror those on Palestinian bodies. The dominant narrative is that Palestinians are barbarous and backwards people. No Palestinian is exempt from it; in fact, Palestinians, as a collective as well as individuals, must forever prove it is inapplicable to them. It is so insidious that it sometimes shows up in ways that, on a cursory look, seem almost approving. Even before the war on Gaza, the most critical description for any Palestinian demonstration in Western media was never its size, or what it aimed to accomplish—but whether it was *peaceful*. That worldview is applied to individuals as much as the collective. A review of my first book in a major newspaper complimented my writing as "calmly civilized," something a person might find notable only if their expectation of a Palestinian is rabid savagery.

Palestinian narratives in the West are thus counternarratives, and forever carry the whiff of subversiveness for that reason. The oppressed exist in an omnipresent parallel with their oppressors. Palestinians are not permitted to be people on their own, outside of their adversariality to Israel. This is a narrative duality that is only applied in one direction; Zionist stories can, and usually do, ignore Palestinian existence, even when it would seem impossible to do so credibly. (Never mind that the duality itself is a false one, omitting many colonial and imperial contexts indispensable to understanding the present.) I remember reading a contemporary novel, about the migration of Soviet Jews to Palestine, that contained virtually no consideration of the Palestinians the migrants displaced to take the land; the influx, in that formulation, became an exclusive concern of the Jews (mirroring, I suppose, the Zionist ideal of statehood). That book became a finalist for the Giller Prize. Meanwhile, someone in my own tight-knit writing group arched their eyebrows over how, in a ten-page short story of mine, the word "Israel" did not come up, as though I must have absentmindedly forgotten that the existence of Palestinian characters is always a contingent one.

From a Zionist perspective, the entanglement is useful. If Palestinian stories are moored to those of Israelis or Jews, it becomes simple for Westerners moulded by decades of narrative—of the victimhood of the Jews, of the barbarity of the Arabs—to pick their side.

The asymmetry of the duality disciplines the stories Palestinians may tell because the expectations of many of those listening to the stories have long been set. Israel and Israelis may act independently, existing in a cone of their own primordial importance, regardless of who is affected by their actions. Meanwhile, Palestinians must always recognize their subordination and only act in accordance with it. Every feature story about the "day after" the Gaza war—how Gaza would be rebuilt, who was to govern it, which of its borders was to open—was primarily about Israel's desires, not those of Palestinians. Stories about Gazans starving to death from the Israeli blockade were always countervailed with paragraphs explaining Israel's counterterrorist aims in closing the borders. It became normal that eating—the ability of a Palestinian to sustain the condition of being alive—was a matter in which Israel had a say. I remember a newspaper once extending me an offer to write for them on the basis that they wanted "more Palestinian voices." Would I be willing to write about how, if Israel goes on bombing the children of Gaza, those children might grow up to hate Israel and terrorize it? In other words, as a Palestinian writer I was expected to centre Israeli potential for trauma as a reason to stop actual and ongoing trauma to Palestinians. When I declined and offered alternative angles, I was told thanks but no thanks.

What we're meant to understand is that Palestinian stories are not our own, in the end. They belong to a kind of governing authority of stories, namely the worldview of empire. If a Palestinian conforms to this worldview, or at least does not disrupt it, they are permitted to tell their story. But if a Palestinian rebels against their assigned position, then their story is silenced, or becomes a niche artefact. If by chance the story bubbles to the mainstream, it will either be met with objection and questioning or is drowned into oblivion. There are ready analogues in other people fighting Western subjugation and oppression. The stories that Black Lives Matter sought to tell (at least in its early stages) were countered by the bulwark of the All Lives Matter movement, whose emergence was a reminder of the heavy infrastructure that Black people have to overcome to be able to narrate their own stories.

Things like this seep into us eventually. We internalize oppressive expectations when we tell our own stories. When every popular conception of you is that of someone in chains, you begin to feel the chains even if they aren't physically there. You narrate yourself, not in spite of the chains, but around them.

I did not approach the Israeli soldier by the exit that day at Allenby. I only eyed him from afar, keeping a lid over the boiling I felt in my heart, because I was conscious of my father sitting next to me. After seven hours of waiting, one of the other soldiers grunted and waved at us to approach, like he was motioning at donkeys. He gave us our documents back and pointed to the entrance gate without a word.

We'd been initiated in hallmark Israeli degradation, but we were in.

That trip was the first (and thus far, only) time I've visited Palestine. Every step my father and I took there was an effort to collect stories of the land, the stories we'd been deprived of all our lives. To integrate into the stories, we made ourselves into almost comically classical conceptions of Palestinians. We retraced what we knew of the movements and lives of our forebears. We went to Salama, the village my grandparents Said and Nima were driven out of, in search of the old family house for which we still had the deed. We tracked down familiar names in other families and met their descendants. We took pictures of random olive trees. We went to Al-Aqsa and prayed. We saw the Mediterranean Sea dance and glint. We tasted the unearthly Palestinian knafeh, interrogating sweets shop owners on their recipes.

Wherever we went, we saw that the Palestine of our mind's eye was one whose body was lacerated all over by the occupation. There were concrete barriers everywhere with armed Israeli soldiers leaning against them, circumscribing our whereabouts. Palestinians were forever made to wait until the order of some soldier permitted them to carry on with their lives. My father and I had the privilege of our new passports, but we understood in our hearts how accidental and unmeaningful that privilege was. It became impossible to think of ourselves apart from those soldiers, because we knew that at any moment, they could stop our trip in its tracks and turn it into something much different, much darker.

The sparse-bearded soldier I had eyed at the border stop was no longer the symbol of my chains, because there were so many other symbols like him, at every point of entry or interest. The differential in power between me and the soldier, and the machine of power he represented, now seemed too vast for my mind to work past. The largeness I sensed in myself before had evaporated. I'd recently read *The Duel* by Chekhov, and I thought of using it as a model to dramatize in fiction an imagined confrontation with that soldier. After two or three days in Palestine, I abandoned the idea. It felt too much like the work of fantasy.

About halfway through our visit to Palestine, my father and I made a day trip to Gaza to see my father's paternal aunt Jameela. It was only recently that we'd discovered we had any family there at all. After my grandfather Said's humiliating flight from Palestine, he hid the existence of his relatives who remained. But in his old age—his post–US passport era—he told my father about Jameela and her family. Like Said, Jameela had trekked down to Gaza from Jaffa during the Nakba. But unlike her brother she remained in Gaza, specifically in the border town of Rafah, where she married and raised a family. Before our trip, my father had telephoned her to introduce himself. At the possibility of meeting her nephew, Jameela unleashed an ululation long and loud enough that I could overhear it from the handset cradled at my father's ear.

It was a forty-five-minute drive from Erez entry point, the highest point in north Gaza, to Rafah at the southern border. I remember so much dust and disorder and poverty in the Gaza streets that our taxi traversed. But another thing I remembered: at least there were no Israeli soldiers eyeing us with guns and distrust.

When we arrived at Jameela's house, a receiving party was waiting for us on some metal chairs outside. Jameela, who looked about seventy, wore a black dress with a chest pattern of red-hued tatreez, a white veil placed flat over her head. She speared the ground with a cane to catapult her out of the chair, waving at the cab driver to stop the vehicle in front of her. Before the sand cloud he kicked up had settled, Jameela had opened the car door and pulled my father out of the back seat by the shoulder pads of his jacket, like she was fetching luggage. She embraced him with an immense smile on her face.

In the next moments my father and I exchanged cheek kisses with so many strangers I felt dizzy and over-scented. Jameela's husband Hisham and her son Hazem were there, with several other men. When we entered the house, even more people emerged. A couple of younger boys immediately began grasping my shoulder and chatting with me. You are our cousin, yes? From America, yes? You know

Hulk Hogan, yes? I noticed how rugged their Arabic was compared to mine, which was rounded and lame from scant use. I noticed the house too. The walls were cracked in most places, and there was cloud-like soot on the paint, in areas where traffic was high. There were piles of clutter covered with blankets, because there was no furniture to stow it away in. My father, in a collared shirt and jacket, stuck out in that environment.

I saw a girl my age coming out from a back room. She had a striking row of beauty marks along one side of her jaw. She wore a hijab, although I felt it may have been a new thing for her, or an optional item—she placed it on without urgency as she was entering the room, her vision landing on me for a second. Either she was hoping I hadn't caught her bare hair or confirming that my eyes couldn't help themselves.

In a room adjoining the kitchen there was already a plastic sheet laid on the floor. There were two cushions on the edge of the sheet, which my father and I were directed to sit on, as though we were the kings of the jalsa. That's when Hazem arrived with the food and placed it on the floor in front of us. It was the classic mansaf, the hill of rice tinted turmeric yellow, with an array of meat arranged on top like a seduction. Jameela tilted a metal bowl over it, unleashing a waterfall of hot yogurt to bathe the rice, a few drops splattering on some of our faces in the process.

115

There was a separate tray of food for the children, and they squeezed around it like iron filings. The girl with the row of beauty marks—her name was Rania, I learned, the neighbours' girl—sat with the children to oversee.

Everyone who ate from those trays on the floor seemed to have the most capable hands, balling the rice and meat in the crook of their fingers and popping it in their mouth in an offhand, cheese-puff sort of way. Their expertise transfixed me, and also disgusted me. The grease that gripped their skin, the granules of rice that sometimes stuck to the webbing between their fingers.

What's wrong, habeebi? Jameela asked me, looking at the end of the tray in front of me, which was untouched. You don't like it?

My father chuckled and nudged me to speak, but Jameela didn't need more clues. Ma'lish, ma'lish, she said, and fished for me a spoon from a pocket in her thawb. I accepted it to a sprinkling of giggles from the children's table.

Between my father and these strangers there was no shortage of things to talk about. They brought up every ancient relation or personage in their respective lives, with each side confirming to the other whether they knew them or not. Jameela must have set off some kind of neighbourhood alarm, because someone new would arrive at the house every few minutes, wiping their hands on their trousers before offering to shake ours. A dozen or so times, Jameela announced with pleasure: It's Dr. Ahmad, my nephew from Amreeka, my brother Said's son.

Hazem, who looked about thirty, planted himself next to my father and peppered him with questions about how to immigrate to America or Canada or even the UK (he wasn't picky). He told him he'd run out of prospects in Gaza and would love it if my father could help him with a change of scenery. Jameela interrupted: You're not going anywhere, Hazem. We need you here. Then she commandeered the subject: Dr. Ahmad—tell us, how is Palestine?

The question should not have surprised me as it did. We may have been the foreigners in that gathering, but as a Gazan, Jameela had never been permitted to see the other side of the country. The Al-Aqsa that we'd unlocked with our American passports was for her family still in the realm of dreams. There are worse prisons than ours, I thought.

At some point came the usual, only half-joking, inquiry about whether I was married yet. I'd rolled my eyes at that sort of thing since I was thirteen, but in that moment, in that place, something about it felt nice, desirable even.

You try to convince him, my father said to his aunt.

A crafty saleswoman, Jameela feigned indifference but said it would not be hard to find a willing young man a good Palestinian wife—dark, pale, in-between, whatever he likes. With a wink, she added: We can always lie and say nice things about him to help the unlucky girl accept.

I thought I heard a cough or something from the children's table, but I didn't dare look. I wondered if the girl with the beauty mark streak would think more highly of me if I had confronted the soldier at Allenby. I wondered if my accent sounded odd to Gazan ears.

I placed my spoon at the edge of the mansaf tray and kneaded some rice into my palm, greasing my fingers all over. I straightened my back into a better posture, something larger.

Halfway through the lunch, Jameela began discussing her plans for the next day. She said it goes without saying that this lunch—the one we were still eating—was unbecoming of us as her guests. It was little more than an hour ago that my father telephoned to tell her we'd made it into Gaza, so she only had time to assemble a meal from whatever she had in the house. Tonight, she promised, Hisham will butcher a sheep from the farm out back, and tomorrow they will invite the entire neighbourhood to lunch in our honour.

My father had experience heading off these types of formalities. 'Amti, our intention was to stay in Gaza for only half a day, he said. There are so many people we have promised to see all over Palestine, and we can't break our commitments. Inshallah we'll come see you and the family more extensively next year.

Jameela acted as if she hadn't heard a word. She replied: I have waited all my life to have relatives. You came, and I was so happy to see you, my brother's own flesh. Now you say you have to leave? I would rather die.

No, no, my father replied. You have to understand our position, 'amti. There is so much we have to do. Plus, we have already taken up too much of your time. Everything was so wonderful today! There really is nothing more you need to do for us.

Jameela gave my father a look that was half humouring, half baleful.

She repeated: I would rather die.

Palestinian stories are slowly coming out of obscurity. The scale of the genocide, and the age we live in, has made it so that whoever used to claim not knowing has forever lost that claim. But as the dominant narrative began to recede behind the evidence of its falsity, Israel and its allies did not stand idle. They understood the importance of pumping fresh narrative into the Western psyche to slow the development of any feelings of remorse about the genocide, or any waning of commitment to the Zionist project.

After the Israeli army invaded and destroyed Al-Shifa Hospital, for example, an army commander assumed the role of media guide by leading for the camera a tour of the premises. He lingered especially on a paper pasted to a wall in the basement, which he claimed listed names of terrorists on shift. It didn't matter that a simple translation of the paper revealed it to be a calendar, listing not shifts, but the Arabic words for the days of the week. The viral message had already been delivered: that Palestinian hospitals are overrun with terrorists, so eliminating them is justifiable.

There was also the pristine, highlighted copy of *Mein Kampf* that one of Israel's chief propagandists, President Isaac Herzog, said that the Israeli army found in a Gazan child's room. It is amusing to think that any Palestinian might require external reading to learn of tyranny and hatred when Israel demonstrates such things to them every day, but the book was a handy prop because of its familiarity to Zionism's Western audiences. The message was that Palestinian children are baptized in the most heinous of thought, so their elimination is justifiable.

There were the clips of Palestinian detainees, bound and blindfolded, the crotches of their pants discoloured with evidence that they'd peed or defecated themselves, as a group of soldiers around them howled with disgust. The message was that Palestinians behave like filthy animals, so their elimination is justifiable.

Then there were the innumerable social media clips of Israeli soldiers laughing themselves to tears as they inspected the lingerie they found in the bedroom closets of Gazan women, sometimes even wearing the flimsy, colourful pieces over their uniforms and engaging in dance or pantomime. It was not clear to me whether the intent was to show Palestinian women as raunchy and dissolute, or to imply that they are not entitled to intimacy, or to simply mortify them by parading about in their private undergarments. Whatever it is, the sexuality of Palestinians was entered into a narrative that made their desires—from the liberatory to the erotic—into something contemptible, an object of laughing derision.

Even if most can now see all these things for the contemptible lies they are, the existence of these narratives is still helpful for Zionist aims. Palestinians are lowered by their very proximity to such concepts as inhumane, animalistic, or degenerate behaviour. The mere association is good enough for the propaganda machine. At first I was surprised by how unbothered, even blithe, Israeli soldiers seemed to be in broadcasting themselves behaving so inhumanely. But it strikes me that the impunity of their narrative of degradation of Palestinians may be intended as a signal, especially to the underinformed. Maybe one tells themselves that a modern, civilized country like Israel (as it is always represented and affirmed) would never do such inhumane things—unless they were warranted. It is a line of thought that can only occur when the Palestinian story is told by their oppressors. As Edward Said has noted, the Palestinian is frequently absent even as stories about them are freely told—they are either physically absent from the scene of the story, or not the one telling it.

A Palestinian who does tell their story is, from the

start, combating a high tide. A counternarrative is in part defined by what it seeks to renounce. A storyteller has to be conscious of the expectations upon them, and disentangle from them before they can actually tell their story. This creates a burden of hyper-intentionality in storytelling that is distinct from (and sometimes unhelpful to) the story itself.

Let's say I tell a story that features a young, angry Palestinian man who does *not* attack an Israeli border soldier. Or a story about a Palestinian child who only has childlike interests, like Hulk Hogan and other wrestling stars. Or a story about an attractive Palestinian woman who is both sexual and chaste. In each of these cases, are these intentional representations that I am making to counter a narrative, or are they truths I cannot help but be interested in? Am I telling a story I want to tell, or am I telling a story that I feel a kind of evangelist burden to tell, as a social corrective? When Adania Shibli writes in *Minor Detail* about the rape of a Palestinian girl by Israeli soldiers in the year after the Nakba, is she crafting an important story that is notable on its own—or is she also doing it in an environment where systemic Zionist sexual aggression is rarely discussed, while allegations of rape perpetrated by Palestinians are a persistent propagandist theme?

A story against narrative is never just told, it is also aware of having been told. As I wrote my first book of fiction, I sometimes had to battle myself to write stories that did not hinge on the canonical conception of what being a Palestinian means. I was torn, for example, between the responsibility to show Palestinian trauma, and my desire to not always write from a place that privileges trauma as a defining feature of a Palestinian life. I worried about the authenticity of my stories if I burdened myself with a sense of responsibility, as opposed to a sense of truth. That both are inextricable clouded my task even more.

Sometimes the expectations are internalized and unconscious. I once wrote a short story about two lovers, one Palestinian and one not. I remember spending weeks drafting the earliest origins of their relationship, even though I knew it was not relevant to the heart of the story. I made the Palestinian partner as sympathetic as possible: low income, hardworking, handsome, intelligent, honourable, et cetera. It was only when I'd reached some thirty pages of writing that I realized what I was doing on a subconscious level: I'd been trying to prove that a Palestinian was worthy of being loved in the first place. My mind had been so thoroughly colonized by Western conceptions that I felt that such work was needed for my narrative to be credible.

The balance between responsibility and truth has only become harder to find after the Gaza war. Even aside from the Israeli hasbara machine and its proxies, in most of today's mainstream narratives Palestinians are objects of either pity or controversy. We witness Palestinians on TV or in newsprint in one of two ways: 1) when they are recounting a horrible tragedy that had been inflicted on them, or 2) when they are trying to explain to a displeased interviewer why they must inconvenience the public with protests.

Palestinian culture or joy rarely come up. It might seem strange to think of such things in the midst of a genocide, when there are graver things to consider. But it shouldn't be strange. Culture and joy bring identification, empathy, and interest. Representations of Zionist joy are commonplace in Western culture, from film to television to literature; that is the reason why the ideology itself, however pernicious to other human beings (both Palestinian and Jewish), is often accepted. When you can laugh with the Zohan, you can more easily tolerate the Zohan's colleagues bulldozing women and children. With scarce exceptions, Palestinians have never been afforded similar positive representations in the media. Palestinian films are never in the mainstream, and Palestinian culture is largely unknown. Where other ethnicities and cultural groups routinely receive significant local airtime for their festivals or celebrations, Palestinian community events in the West languish for years without coverage, absent some manufactured controversy or other.

Sometimes, the only really acceptable Palestinian is the one who is willing to divorce their identity, or at least minimize it. A type like DJ Khaled may come to mind in this respect. As for me, I think a lot about an audience member who attended a literary lecture I gave about my first book. During the question period, she rose to ask—in a manner that suggested she was trying to help me—whether I would consider writing something that is just *normal*, that isn't about being Palestinian. I suppose that after slogging through my book, she felt that enough was enough, and now I should use whatever talent I possessed on something other than my usual parochial material.

It seems I wasn't the only one who felt the burden of societal expectations when it came to Palestinians. My audience felt it, too, and sometimes they preferred if I joined them in escaping, in looking away.

We were offered no escape from Rafah.

Jameela had given us the parameters of our detainment. We would stay the night at her house, and then we were free to leave tomorrow, after the lunch feast she had planned. She framed it as a compromise: her preference was that we remain a month or two, that my father build a house next to hers, and that I marry someone from the neighbourhood. She was not prepared to accept abbreviating all that into a half-day visit.

My father argued and argued with his aunt. He couldn't leave without her blessing, but Jameela would not give it. He began to panic. He pulled out his appointment book to show her all the names of people he had already committed to seeing elsewhere in Palestine. "Look at this page: What will I tell Dr. Suroor in Bethlehem—I'm supposed to meet him tonight! What will I tell Dr. Balqees in Beit Jala, she's tomorrow!"

And yet for every person he mentioned, Jameela countered with another person in Gaza that we would be forgoing if we left. It was a strange argument to witness. My father's love for people meant that every time Jameela offered him the string of someone's story, my father was too curious not to pull on it. He'd ask question after question, only to realize that doing so meant Jameela was winning the argument. At some point, Jameela became so confident of her victory that even as my father was entreating her, she began instructing her children on preparations for the next day. Boy, you head to the grocer and get the eggplant and cauliflower we will need for tomorrow, and pass by so-and-so's house to tell them they're invited. Girl, go get your brothers' room ready for the guests—change the linens and mop the floor.

Eventually Jameela's husband Hisham and her son Hazem prevailed on my father to quit. Neither of them had yet won a battle with Jameela, and my father should not harbour ambitions of being the first. Hisham took us outside to cool off.

As we passed through the hallway, I thought I heard Rania, the neighbours' girl, speaking a few words in broken English. I wondered if she was practicing for my benefit.

I'm not one to enjoy spending much time with strangers, but I thought it would not be the worst thing if we had to stay the night in Rafah.

Outside, we sat on the metal folding chairs, their vinyl backing torn and the foam busting out of them. All around us was Rafah's desert. Jameela's house was not in a heavily populated area, so we could see most ways around. There was a small hill in the distance. Behind it is Egypt, Hisham said.

Is that where the refugee tents used to be, in the old days? my father asked.

Hisham poured us tea from a kettle blackened with use. No, that's the other way, he said, but you can see it from behind the mountain for sure. There's no tents anymore, the camp is mostly buildings now.

Jameela called her husband from inside the house. He ducked in, and there I could see them talking in a low voice. I saw Jameela gesturing at the animal enclosure out back. There was one scrawny sheep, bleating every once in a while.

Is that the one, do you think? my father asked me, craning his neck to see. The only other creatures there were three chickens ambling about. That was it. So Jameela and her family, which we could tell were not well-off, were going to butcher their one remaining sheep in our honour.

A breeze developed in the day, and a few cumulus clouds shielded us from the sun for a bit. Jameela came out to have her tea with us. My father seemed ready to say something but thought better of it. The pair of them took their tea together mostly in silence.

Jameela asked if my father wanted an afternoon nap. My father said he did, but that he wanted to take me on a walk first, to show me the border with Egypt.

Oh yes, Jameela said, you boys should see where Said and Nima made camp. She started pointing with her cane where we should go.

My father and I got up and walked toward that area, which was only a couple hundred yards away. My father huffed as he scaled up the gentle incline of the hill. There were a few UNRWA signs here and there pointing to the refugee camp.

When we reached the other side of the hill, my father looked around. At the time I knew little of my grandparents' time in Rafah, or the awfulness they experienced there. But the place still felt important. It was where my ancestors had experienced the biggest fork in the story that our family would tell in the future.

We heard the sheep bleat again. From our distance it was faint as rustling leaves. My father felt in his breast pocket for his appointment book.

He took a deep, uncertain breath.

Listen, Saeed, he said. Now . . . Now, we run.

— — —

In the wake of the Gaza war, trauma has overtaken Palestinian stories to a near-total extent, more than ever before. By far the most common Palestinian story in the public consciousness now is the obituary.

In most cases we have only heard the stories of Palestinians *because* of the horror of their endings. The final outcome has become the event that imbues relevance on the life lived before it. Hind Rajab was an adorable five-year-old girl who loved her family—we did not know her, until she was shot to death in her family's car while she, terror-stricken and inconsolable, was on the phone with aid workers. The Palestinian death story has become so commonplace as to sometimes be recursive: Sha'ban al-Dalou was an immaculately-kempt teenager who played guitar—we did not know him until he was burned alive, holding the cord of his IV in the tent he built for his displaced family on the grounds of a hospital. Mahasen al-Khateeb was a bright artist and designer, who commemorated Sha'ban al-Dalou with an illustration of his horrific final moments—we did not know her until she was killed by an airstrike on her neighbourhood in Jabalia the day after she published the illustration.

There is a familiarity to the arc, an inevitability. The stories themselves are told to make a point. Palestinians, like other cultures, honour their dead by speaking of them and remembering them. For people whose pain has long been hidden, it is even more necessary to tell those stories. But the predictability of a Palestinian's untimely death is not a feature of the stories, but a prerequisite to be permitted to tell them. A Palestinian who has not been killed, or at least suffered a killing in their family, is one whose story is not story enough. For the West, the death arc has come to define whether a life is worth talking about. Without this final trauma their relevance to our discourse—their very Palestinianness—decreases. During the war, I remember many media members who asked me, in pre-interviews or introductory emails, if I had family or friends affected by the onslaught on Gaza, fervently burrowing for ways to inject the quote or two they hoped to get from me with the gravity of proximate trauma.

Usually a Palestinian's end has already arrived by the time their story is told, but sometimes the end is merely impending. Gazan poet Refaat Alareer's poem "If I Must Die" gained readership in the early days of the genocide. Underlying its popularity is that the poet foretold his own death. Here was a Palestinian who understood his story— because it was the story of many like him—and asked that it be remembered after he is killed. When he was duly assassinated by Israel in December 2023, the poem catapulted to worldwide renown and was translated into scores of languages. But does part of its popularity stem from the fact that the story it tells—and the poet's aware-ness of that story—so perfectly fits the trauma we believe is a defining feature of being Palestinian? I love the poem, yet I don't quite know the answer to that question.

Being defined by our limits is not just a problem of outside perception; it impacts our stories themselves. I have thought about how characters of other identities are allowed, in life and in literature, to have nuanced and subtle preoccupations, moments of understanding, or quiet reflection. Literature is built on stories like that, and so are more mundane genres like the Sunday features pages. We understand that there is an endless range of human feeling and experience, and we seek it. But this range is not one on which Palestinians are often situated.

All of our lives, Palestinian or not, are temporary. But when life is memorialized mainly for its extinguishment, it drains it of meaning even as it is being lived. When our story arcs always end in death, we are concretized as dead people in waiting. We should never forget that this is a product of the cruelty of the oppressor. More than just normalizing the killing of Palestinians, it has rendered their killing a baseline requirement for generating pathos. Without it, the story does not feel complete or noteworthy, at least according to the expectations we have developed. We are not satisfied—on the level of story—until Palestinians are dead.

A requirement like that makes it difficult to imagine other arcs. Because death is the most crushing conclusion, and the one for which audiences are most breathless, other conclusions feel unfit for the telling.

Now, we run, he said.

My father has always been portly and unathletic. On the rare occasions he ran—to get out of rainfall, or to pretend to chase a small child—he played those few seconds off as high comedy. But that day in Rafah my father ran like I've never seen him run before. He ran with his arms extended down, flopping back and forth as if he were a boat and they were his oars. Yalla Saeed, faster, faster! he said. I jogged next to him, confused, trying not to drift too far ahead.

This way, he ordered, panting. Stay on this line! I realized he was trying to remain hidden behind the hill.

After a minute he could barely breathe and had to stop. He held his sides from exhaustion. We could see a taxi in the distance, parked outside one of the border houses. Okay, okay, okay, he said, steeled by the sight. And he dashed again.

When we reached the cab, my father teared up from the pain in his chest. Ya rab! he said. I told the alarmed driver not to worry, and we got in.

Fifteen minutes later, my father finally regained his breath. His jacket was spotted with sweat and his shirt had come out of his pants.

He explained to me that he could not bear to let Jameela's family slaughter their one sheep for us. He just couldn't. That family needed the sheep more than we needed to be honoured. He would not permit the feast to happen. As soon as we were out of Gaza, he would telephone to let Jameela know we left. Her intransigence had given him no choice.

The explanation made sense to me, and I appreciated his protectiveness of his aunt's finances. As the taxi blew through Gaza's roads, I wanted to say something light about how funny it was that we ran. But my father did not look in the mood for that at all. He was unsettled, like he was unsure what to do with himself.

I don't like running away like fugitives the way we did, he said after a while. He gazed out the window. I just feel . . . *small*, he said.

Now, many years later, my father's turn of phrase makes me think of the largeness that I saw in myself that day at Allenby. It had not been just a macho conception of physical size, although that was how it manifested in my mind as a young adult male. The largeness was really a signifier of the capability I felt in myself. I felt capable of returning, a prospect that was especially tantalizing in light of my diasporic inferiority complex. I felt a capability to demonstrate that our history and indigeneity to the land counted for something, for everything. I felt so large that I believed I could overcome the soldiers and their weapons.

That largeness was, of course, almost all imagined. Like my father's youthful poems, it was a story I was telling myself, about who I am, and what I can be. It was a story of me being too large for the strictures and expectations on us as Palestinians.

Yet my father felt small. He'd obviously been overwhelmed. For years, he had not even known *of* this aunt, never mind her family or neighbourhood. But now that he'd visited her, there was a whole other world open to him. Jameela was not only bursting with love for him, she was also eager to infuse him with all her relatives and their stories. In this world of newness my father wasn't just a proximate character, but a key one. It may be that, amid all these new stories, my father didn't know what he could absorb and what he couldn't afford to even try to absorb.

I believe that when we have people's stories, we are responsible for them. The closeness we form to others through their stories makes us their keepers—not just of the stories, but of the people themselves. We owe them care and understanding. And if they have our stories, they are our keepers too.

My father loved people, down to his core. But how many lives could he afford to feel so close to?

At the beginning of the Gaza war, I, like many others around the world, took it as a personal mission to elevate as many stories from Gaza as I could. The least I could do was elevate people that Western society had deemed to be beneath humanity. I shared and shared. Early on, this felt like important work, the process of building awareness that precedes the shifting of the narrative. (If I'm honest, it also helped me to feel like I was suffering *with* the Gazans somehow, as much as my suffering paled in comparison to theirs.)

The stories I shared were of people at likely the very worst moments in their lives: a toddler covered with bomb debris and writhing in fear, or a doctor doing her job in a hospital only to stumble across her own child dead on one of the stretchers. Even the most hardened mind can crumple against its best efforts sometimes. I longed for a story I shared to cause a crumpling in someone who had otherwise made up their mind against Palestinians.

But after about six or seven months, I was sure there was no one on the planet who was still unaware of what was happening, even if all the algorithms had been re-configured on the fly to suppress and marginalize. There seemed to be a new acceptance that while the situation was bad, there was nothing to be done about it. A common behavioural pattern had developed: view a horror clip from Gaza, then placidly swipe on to a recipe video or a viral dance. Gaza was a new, grisly genre of content, but just content nonetheless.

Eventually, I felt the Gazans and their stories—particularly in their frank, pictorial forms—were too dear to me to display, like some street seller, in the hope of moving someone. Before he was killed, Alareer had viewed it as both selfish and treacherous to keep stories to yourself, but maybe he hadn't seen enough of the world's reaction to the genocide to disabuse him of that notion. Telling the stories began to feel, to me anyway, not just unworthwhile, but exploitative. I felt I was cheapening the people in them even more so than the dominant narrative had already cheapened them. I stopped sharing. The narrative had to change, but I could not let myself *use* these human beings, who I cherished so much even if they were mostly strangers, as instruments for such change.

Whatever power stories possessed, I felt we had reached its limit.

And if that was the case with stories of overwhelming horror and poignancy, what chance then did the smaller, more ordinary stories have?

My father and I made it back to the Erez exit in that taxi, then crossed from Gaza back to the West Bank an hour later. Did my father call his aunt Jameela, as he'd planned? Did Jameela see through whatever excuse he gave her to understand that he was only trying to spare the family an unnecessary cost? What became of Rania, the girl with the beauty marks? Did I really catch her eye? Did I inquire about her after the trip? Did Hazem get to immigrate to America after all, and did he prosper? What became of the young boys who were so eager to talk to me? Their names were Ayad and Tareq, by the way—or at least, those were the pseudonyms I gave them like I gave all the Gazans in this chapter, my piddling measure of guarding them.

In that group of human beings my father and I met that day, there were countless stories of sadness, of joy, of understanding, of reversal, of Joycean epiphany, of haphazardness, of slapstick, of complexity, of denouement.

I've told a tiny fraction of those stories, but the vast majority of them I have not. And since the time I was there, Gaza has suffered numerous cycles of attacks. That group has accumulated many more stories: told, untold, and unknown.

But they are too dear to me, these people, to talk of their endings.

– 5 –

Platform and Safety

If nothing else, Israel and its promulgators have shown themselves to be strong students of history, or at least certain history. They must have admired the work of the Crusaders ransacking Constantinople and destroying the Imperial Library of the Byzantines. They must have read about the Mongols dumping tomes from Baghdad's library, the House of Wisdom, into the Tigris River, tinging its waters ink-black. They must have marveled at the panache of the Spanish Inquisition burning Arabic texts in a big bonfire at the Plaza de Bib-Rambla in Granada, on the orders of the Archbishop of Toledo. And they must have grudgingly understood the sagacity of Nazi students heaving into flames some twenty-five thousand "un-German" books—especially those of Jewish and pro-Jewish writers like Bertolt Brecht, Sigmund Freud, and Thomas Mann—in an effort to end the "decadence and moral corruption" that Joseph Goebbels said emanated from such works.

These learnings were put into practice right away during the Nakba in 1948, when the Zionist militias, doing extra credit work on top of their main task of indigenous dispossession, looted some seventy thousand books and manuscripts relating to Palestinian history and culture, destroying much of them. We know that, today, such cultural destruction has become a matter of demonstrated priority. Within the first month of the Gaza war, Israeli bombs had leveled the Samir Mansour Library, the largest bookshop and publisher in Gaza. The bookshop housed hundreds of thousands of books, much of them devoted to Palestinian writing. It was in close proximity to three universities, making it a hub for students. In an assault that left few edifices undestroyed, it might be hard to distinguish what is targeted from what is merely included. But this was the second campaign in which the Samir Mansour library was hit—the first time, during Israel's assaults in 2021, it was wiped out completely. The owners rebuilt and reopened it in 2022, only for Israel to destroy it once more in 2023.

I think of the bookshop because it is so strictly concerned with the written word. But learning as a whole was a target: Israel leveled all twelve of Gaza's universities during the war. This represented a progression from the intifada years, when Israel had contented itself with merely shuttering all of the West Bank's universities.

Not that erasure takes the form of outright destruction only. Israel's list of banned books numbers in the thousands. The vast majority of these books are Palestinian stories, or histories challenging Israel's permissible thought lines. Israeli soldiers have for decades routinely stopped Palestinian schoolchildren on their way to school to rifle through their bags in search of a book with offending material—for example, a picture of a Palestinian flag—to confiscate. (Post-October 7, these practices were upgraded to just shooting the child altogether, since the child's mind is likely beyond banning-based rehabilitation anyway.)

During the war, Al Jazeera was the lone international news broker that derived news from Palestinian sources or carried Palestinian narratives with any consistency. The Israeli military leveled Al Jazeera's Gaza office in one of its first acts, and later ventured into the West Bank to shut down its Ramallah office too. The Israeli government unanimously sanctioned *Haaretz*, the Israeli newspaper most dubious of the genocide. During the war, Israel banned thousands of newspaper articles from appearing in domestic papers on the grounds that they were too damaging at too sensitive a juncture. This wasn't a novel strategy, but an escalation of Israel's usual practices in calmer times. Few of the banned stories ever trickle out, even after many years have passed. Still, as the Gaza war entered its second year, the Israeli government recognized that its narratives had become undermined by its genocidal actions. In response, it increased its investment in "consciousness warfare" twenty-fold, funding that it diffuses into the public via cultural icons, social media influencers, professional hasbarists, and Zionist groups in the West and elsewhere.

Maybe it's a nod to Palestinians' status as highly educated people that their cultural, educational, and news institutions have always been targets. When the literate are oppressed, they always resort to books, because that's where the loneliness of their misery finds companionship, and where their despair can be quelled by understanding and triumphing in the experiences of others. The feelings of discovery, enrichment, and spiritual victory that come over us in bookstores, libraries, or universities reaffirm a precious part of our humanity. When they are wiped out, that part of us is affected deeply. I remember being sad for days after discovering a secondhand bookstore I once frequented in Montreal had closed down. Places like this are precious because by unlocking for us the narratives of others, they are really birthplaces for our own narratives.

But however catastrophic the loss of institutions may be, they can always be rebuilt—books can be reprinted, and bricks can once again be slathered with mortar. The main problem that must be solved by anyone taking a serious go at genocide is the persistence of blatant cultural acts by the survivors. The best way to address that is by targeting the producers of culture themselves, whose maddening vocation is creating more and more of it.

At its core it is a power play. Michel Foucault said that power is not solely a product of force, but also of discourse and knowledge production—knowledge and power cannot be separated or considered apart from each other. As vessels of cultural knowledge, Palestinian artists are natural targets for anyone intending to strip Palestinians of power. All of a culture cannot be erased without a completist version of annihilation, but the strongest vestiges of that culture can be erased by erasing the artist.

I am uncomfortable around discussions of what should or shouldn't be the role of the artist. Having said this, it seems to me that, as a general matter, an artist's strongest characteristic is rarely some kind of deep political acumen. But the artist is almost by definition a humanist. This means they have the potential to slash past the political and instead prioritize human values. They can think of core qualities like dignity and security, even in the midst of cacophonies of politicized excuse-making and prevarications.

It's also important that the artist's work exists in the public sphere. There could be a thousand private conversations about how awful a situation is, but the work of the artist can make those conversations a matter of public discourse. It's not just about having the ability to do so, via whatever platform they may have; it is also about willingness. Often the main service that the artist provides is temerity. A certain kind of artist is compelled to say the unsayable because they cannot bear *not* expressing the truth as they know it. They are the witness that has not been prevailed upon—by concerns for their safety, or for their reputation—not to enter the witness stand of the public. And the temerity of the artist inaugurates and encourages temerity in the masses. This kind of artist is different from one that witnesses only so that they can throw their hands up, besieged by tragedy but resigned to being unable to cause any real change. In the hands of the unresigned artist, art becomes a form of political action, even while maintaining its form and function as art.

This is especially important in vacuums of political capacity, like in the West where pro-Palestinian political action is forbidden or rejected, or in Israel with its crackdown on the Palestinian identity. Artists are uniquely positioned to take on the enormity of entrenched power relationships, and via their work foment further action. This can be a key step in eroding the legitimacy of regimes.

It seems to me that the body of the artist is significant here. The body is what goes in public to display or read their work, and discuss the ideas in their work, or even their ideas outside the work. The artist's body becomes a kind of bulwark, a physical entity defending an idea, embodying it.

Such potential for a physical disruption of power is terrifying for the oppressor. A cultural avatar for nascent political action must be destroyed with no less urgency than the political or military leaders. Historically, Israel has been clear about this motivation. Ghassan Kanafani is but one Palestinian writer whose literary work became inextricable from his political activities. The Mossad eventually assassinated him, together with his young niece, via a bomb planted in his car, in 1972 in Beirut, where he had been exiled. Later that same year, the Mossad also assassinated the writer Wael Zwaiter, who had also been active politically, in his exile in Rome, where he was in the midst of a project translating *One Thousand and One Nights* into Italian.

Such tactics persist to this day. I do not believe it was a coincidence that Refaat Alareer was assassinated not long after "If I Must Die" gained popularity, and his social media reach as a transmitter of culture increased. In fact, Israel seemed more adept at (and arguably more focused on) killing leading writers than leading Hamas figures. Within three months of the Gaza war, Israel had killed Alareer as well as the writers Saleem Al-Naffar, Inas al-Saqa, Mustafa Al-Sawwaf, Nour El Din Adnan Hajjaj, Heba Abu Nada, and many others. Meanwhile, it took Israel over a year to kill Yahya Al-Sinwar, and even that seemed to have happened by accident, as the Hamas leader had opted to act like a foot soldier and engage in combat with Israeli soldiers and drones, even after one of his arms had been severed.

When I wrote my first book, the collection of stories *Her First Palestinian*, I did not do so motivated by a sense of nationalism or revolutionary fervor. I did not believe I was going to be an instrument of liberation, or education, or even (if I'm honest) the exploration of serious issues. "I am no proselytizer," asserts the protagonist of my title story, and on that point he was a mouthpiece for me. My sole motivation for writing was my love of language and stories. That my characters were Palestinian was a product of my background and my immediate environment; I couldn't very well write *Her First Croat*.

Even so, I knew it was likely my book would be considered another exemplar of ethnographical Palestinian writing. My impulse was to resist that. I never thought that Chekhov's works were about Russianness, even if he almost always wrote about Russians and Russia. So, when I submitted my finished manuscript I had attached a different title to it, one that was much less signaling—before my shrewd editor Shirarose Wilensky suggested to me otherwise. In my early interviews I downplayed, where I could, the Palestinian aspects of my work in favour of some larger universality of human experience.

This attitude was due in part to my disinclination, both nurtured and natural, to put forward ethnicity as the defining feature of my personality. When the book was published, I was in my forties. I had settled into a life where I did not hide my background, but I did not emphasize it either. I thought I'd achieved a delicate balance of being myself without requiring people to always reckon with all of what myself might entail for them. To me, the proof of my success on this front was that my former workplace, a large white-shoe law firm on Toronto's Bay Street, asked if I would do a book talk for them.

I'd enjoyed a pleasant career at the firm. I was hired there while I was still a law student, and it was the first place where I felt a modicum of professional belonging. The feeling was rooted in the odd solidarity of overstressed lawyers toiling in the trenches of big law. Like many, I absorbed the culture of grueling hours and ready destruction of my personal life for the sake of work. I even savoured it sometimes. I remember occasions when, working on a file until almost dawn, I would wander the deserted halls of the firm, my dress shoes mercifully off, feeling a sense of disturbed pride in my obvious commitment.

In the eight years I spent at the firm, I did not tell anyone I was Palestinian, except on two or three occasions when specifically asked. Not that it didn't come out. I had made it an annual tradition to host a party for my coworkers at my downtown apartment. I started it as a way for each year's cohort of timid students to mingle with the firm's associates. Having freshly taken off their shoes at the door, people would come in and see on my walls a large reproduction of the famous "Visit Palestine" poster (1936, Tourist Development Association of Palestine), featuring a shady tree as a frame for a vista that included the Wailing Wall and the Dome of the Rock—an item that my brother had purchased from an art shop in Old Jerusalem and gifted to me. Some would remark on it to start a conversation, and some would stew in their new knowledge about their host. For those nights I also prepared a large spread of Palestinian food—hummus, muhammara, fatteh, zaatar manakeesh. Every now and then I innovated with handheld musakhan bites, to avoid the big oily mess of the genuine article getting all over my furniture via the hands of my guests. I feigned busyness with my hosting duties, but I often listened keenly to any chatter about what I'd made, eager to interject with tidbits of history or culture if the opportunity presented itself. As the night advanced, when my apartment reached peak congestion, I'd unveil my pièce de résistance: a pan or two of homemade knafeh, drowning both in syrup and in my glorification of this legend of Palestinian confectionery.

The divide between work and home was important to me: I was fine to be a diligent cipher professionally, but if you chose to come to my home, I was unwilling to minimize myself.

I left the firm on amicable terms, having formed many strong friendships, some of which persist to this day. But away from the all-consuming chaos of big law, and aided by the restrictions on socialization during the pandemic, I was able to write again. My book was published three years after I left the firm, but it felt like even less. So I was delighted when a group of my former colleagues contacted me to ask if I'd be interested in coming back to the firm for a day to talk about the book.

The proposed event would be a reading followed by a Q&A led by moderators selected from the firm's lawyers. It would be positioned as part of the firm's Diversity, Equity, and Inclusion (DEI) efforts for that year; there already was a DEI book club, and the organizers thought my book would be a natural fit. A date was set, and the event was advertised to lawyers and staff. I was asked to name a speaking fee but wouldn't hear of it.

From my experience, big-firm lawyers usually have to be semi-forcibly rounded up at the last minute to attend any nonessential events, if only to avoid embarrassing the speaker with a paltry crowd. But for my event, enthusiastic RSVPs piled up quickly to such levels that larger and larger spaces had to be found. Many at the firm messaged me to express two very specific categories of excitement about it. For people whose lives take place largely within the confines of the office, the idea that someone like them could have any fruitful side venture (especially writing a book) was wild. Others felt a different kind of thrill: that one could broach, in the office, issues of real challenge to society as it was currently configured, like Palestine and Palestinians. The more usual DEI topics—about equity for gay and lesbian communities, for example—serve mostly as box-checking exercises, reminders of things most everyone agreed on already. This was something different.

It was a thrill for me, too. For a first-time author, the world of book tours felt like a sugary fantasyland of affirmation, but this stop, at this law firm, was special because it was a moment of melding for my previously divided life. The enthusiastic response was particularly touching. I remember a few minutes here and there where I pictured myself as some kind of revenant hero. The mind flies sometimes, I suppose.

In the West, killing authors is not yet encouraged, and until recent years, wholesale book bannings have largely been considered déclassé. However, the next best alternatives in the field of suppression are widely practiced. One of the most reliable is canceling the appearances of writers, artists, or other figures of perceived or actual activism. Stretching back decades, there are scarcely any Palestinian writers in the West that have not been canceled due to their identity or the nature of their work. In the fall of 2023, the muscle memory of suppression was flexed anew with greater determination. Adania Shibli's lecture at Frankfurt Book Fair was immediately canceled after the Hamas strike. Talks by Mohammed el-Kurd and Emily Jacir were canceled, as were ones by non-Palestinian critics of Israel like Viet Thanh Nguyen and Masha Gessen. The reason for the cancellation was rarely given with any clarity or consistency, but the message it delivered was obvious. Palestinians and their allies may not be platformed in either one of two divergent contexts: a) in the wake of other Palestinians revolting against Israel; or b) in the midst of Israel annihilating Palestinians.

Canceling is an institutional act. To the extent that inviting someone to speak represents the institution seeking their viewpoint, canceling them represents the institution deeming their viewpoint no longer palatable. With rare exceptions, the author themselves will have done nothing between the time of their invitation to the time of their canceling that would account for the change of heart. The cancellation is instead a response to internal or external pressures (real or perceived) upon the institution, pressures it deems significant enough to deny a previously solicited exercise of speech. The institution considers what the canceled writer *would* have said, and even what they represent in the mere presence of their body, to be a potential peril to its funding or to the views of its stakeholders, or both.

I believe that Palestinian writers are perceived to be a

danger precisely because their power is not derived from violence or weapon-based intimidation, which are usually frowned upon as methods of communication in civil society. Their danger is that they practice a value protected by countries founded on constitutionally enshrined freedoms. As habitual, and in some cases masterful, exercisers of speech, artists are untenable risks. It is not just that their message itself might change minds, or that the message becomes easier to accept when the artists lend it their credibility. It's that the artist appearing in front of strangers, evincing thoughtfulness or humour or fury or whatever appealing characteristic they may have, becomes closer to their audience, less alien and ignorable.

It would not have been unexpected or even irrational if the Western populace's response to their governments' support of a lawless, genocidal regime were domestic violence and destruction. But this was not how artists responded. Instead, they spoke up. The artist may speak from a place of extreme rage, but importantly, she speaks, rather than destroy property or threaten lives. That exercise of freedoms commonly celebrated in the West is particularly galling, because it means that the artist—and all the people the artist represents—share the values of the West. It is more difficult to go through with extermination if the targets seem so alike to you. If someone were exposed to the words of Fadwa Tuqan, for but one example, I don't think they could bear to kill her kin.

The ostracization of canceling isn't just about depriving the artist of a platform they earned by virtue of their work. The canceled artist now wears the scarlet letter of a pariah. Those in their potential audience who may have been exposed to a different viewpoint by listening to the artist now accrue a newfound suspicion of them and their message, and may even feel relieved that they were spared from exposure to them. Even if the artist were speaking to their own community—for example, a writer speaking to other writers at a prize ceremony for writing—even in those cases, the cancellation crystallizes a divide in the community with respect to the artist. Members of the community are now forced to choose sides. And so in many minds the artist's name is now preceded by the tacit adjective of *controversial.*

Where before, the institution that invited the artist had de facto lent them some of their legitimacy, even championed them, cancellation means that the artist now stands more alone than ever before. They become the only remaining target of the harassment that had been awakened by their scheduled appearance, even more so if the artist dares to complain about what happened to them or makes it a public issue. Their inboxes then become a site of vitriol, their personal lives subject to doxxing, targeting, and worse. Whatever power they had is not only stripped away by the cancellation, it's been undermined even more by institutional discrediting. Their reputations become disputatious, fringe.

Artists who do speak out for Palestine understand the danger they are in. It became de rigueur that artist-led events against the genocide withhold until the last possible moment essential information, like scheduled time, location, participants, and even whether the event would take place at all. The risk of harassment and physical intimidation was simply too great. Online risks were especially insidious. I was the target of several attempts at discovering my contacts and location via Palestine-specific phishing on messaging platforms. It is not a coincidence that the majority of people tracked by the well-known anti-Palestinian doxxing sites are students, artists, and intellectuals—all of them bearers of cultural knowledge in some form.

The result is to create an environment of fear. The canceled artist lives in fear and suspicion of their environment, of the institutions that invite them, of the consequences of consenting to speak out, and sometimes of the things they want to say. Their potential audience is injected with fear of the artist, the artist's message, and the artist's identity. The institution fears losing its funding and credibility, and fears inviting similar artists in the future, lest doing so instigates another public relations blow-up. Even those who complained and lobbied against the artist have now had their alleged fears institutionally validated, confirming that they *should* continue to live in avoidance of viewpoints that conflict with theirs.

None of these issues are limited to artists, of course.

We have seen doctors experience them, as well as jour-
nalists, lawyers, politicians. Anyone who chooses to speak
has to deal with a laser dot of risk trained on their body.
What distinguishes artists, for me, is that they are among
those most ready to take it on.

Do you have time to speak?

I received this one-line email as I was driving through
downtown Toronto on a rainy October afternoon, my car
slipping and sliding on the wet street. It was from one
of the event organizers at my former law firm. I had exchanged a few emails with them in recent weeks, about
this or that logistical issue that needed ironing out, so a
request for a conversation, presumably to expedite things,
did not surprise me. I found an underground parking lot,
checked my cell phone reception, and took the call.

Hi Saeed, it's so great to hear your voice!

Instead of my contact on the other line, it was a cloy-
ing, singsong voice I did not immediately recognize. The
woman introduced herself as the head of DEI at the firm.
This both jogged my memory of her and also should have
been my first clue.

Saeed, thanks so much for getting on the line so
quickly. How are you! Oh my goodness, let me just start
by saying we are so, *so* excited about the success of your
book. We have been monitoring with such joy the acco-

lades it's receiving already. You know, we still think of you as one of our own, and we could not be more proud!

Years ago I had maybe nodded at this person in the hall once or twice.

Okay, I replied. Thank you very much, that's very kind. What's up?

Well as I said, we are so proud, and so very excited about your great achievements. The reason I'm calling is that, as you know, we have an event scheduled with you that's coming up soon. I just wanted to let you know personally—and I want you to know this is not what any of us wanted—but just to say that we will not be able to host your event any longer.

At first I couldn't quite follow, so I reiterated what I heard. Wait, am I understanding you right that you're canceling the event? Is that what you mean? Can you tell me why?

Well, first of all, Saeed, what I would *hate* is for you to feel put out by this, at all. You really should not be at all! But it's just that recently we received some concerns from some of our lawyers, and we think—

What kind of concerns?

Well, this is of course by no means intended to reflect anything about you, or your book. But the concerns we have heard are that an event like this could endanger the psychological safety of some members of our firm. That's what it boils down to. I know you, as a lawyer yourself, appreciate we have to take that sort of thing seriously. So, what makes the most sense in light of everything is to no longer have the event. It goes without saying that we continue to watch with admiration your achievements and will always root for you! I think I speak for many when I say . . .

I was too stunned to remember what I managed in response. I might've lingered on the words *psychological safety*, because lingering on words is a primary mode of mine. Questions began to precipitate, too quickly for me to disentangle them in real time. Who were those complainants? Who made the decision to cancel? How am *I* a danger?

But my pride was too injured to ask anything else in that moment. Instead, for the first time in my life, I hung up on someone mid-sentence.

In the underground lot where I was parked, engine still running, there were some people fiddling with the ticket machine outside. I watched them, for what felt like eons, until they finally figured out how to get the machine to accept one of their credit cards. Then they finally left.

That's when I slammed my hands against my steering wheel, over and over, angrier than I'd been in a long time. This was in the fall of 2022, almost a year before the start of the Gaza war. It was the first time I was canceled.

I remember sitting in that parking lot defending myself in my mind. I was not some stranger to this firm. I was not an outsider with an agenda, or a loose cannon, or even an enigma that is better off discarded to avoid the potential for surprises. I began my law career at that firm, worked there for years. I participated in countless social events and student recruitment drives. I ate horrible Bay Street takeout on the weekends with other lawyers working on major files. I never allowed myself to utter a stray word of hurt to anyone.

But now I had been specifically told not to show up at the firm. I was unwelcome and unwanted. My presence would be—and I couldn't stop thinking of this word—a *danger* to my former colleagues.

I suppose I was also shocked because I hardly considered myself as some symbol of Palestine or something. I was just an obscure short story writer. The thought that my fictions could hurt the psychology of some of the most powerful lawyers in the country was risible. (Although if their concerns were sincere, I wasn't without sympathy for them; imagine how difficult it must be to hide such delicate constitutions from the clients that pay them ludicrous amounts to stand on their behalf in front of judges and CEOs.)

The most acute feeling I had in those first moments was not shock, anger, frustration, or even bafflement. It was shame. The feeling had multiple dimensions. I was ashamed that now everyone at the firm would think their former colleague is an unsavoury character, someone with views that can't be countenanced in a mainstream setting.

I was also ashamed that, by writing a book with characters of my heritage, I had evidently outed myself as a closeted bigot, after having spent so much of my life devising cunning ways to avoid letting the secret out. I knew this was a preposterous thing to feel, but I was mortified anyway. On that day I was still too naive to understand that the cost of creating authentic art is isolation—and as a Palestinian, the cost is multiplied several times over. Instead, I felt like I had failed to navigate my life properly. I felt foolish, like I should have known better.

The feeling of foolishness made me remember an incident from long ago, with my father. When I told him I was applying to law school, my father had been elated. My decision reawakened in him the desire to brag about me, which I had forced into retreat by my years of distance and directionlessness. I remember one gathering in particular, a formal occasion at our family home in Mississauga. My father, having by then built his life back up completely, prided himself on wearing crisp, generous-fitting suits when we were entertaining. For the occasion, he put on a new tie, which he turned over for me before the guests arrived to show me its Italian label.

My father adored gatherings. When it got late enough that his conversation started to flag, my father, tired but still enjoying himself, would often clap his nearest seated guest on the leg and tell them how much he enjoyed their company.

My son is going into law, you know, he told one of his visitors that night. The visitor in question was a lawyer himself, the firstborn of an Arab family we'd been friends with for a long time. He was still young—about my age— but already his reputation was that of an unstoppable force of success. His suits, with their peacock-loud patterns and vacuum-pack fit, were rumoured to have never known a store rack. Many in our local community put him on a tier of respect uncommon for such a young person, and my father was no exception.

What do you think? he asked our visitor, grasping his knee and pulling close to him, like he was asking for an earnest opinion, man to man. Would my son make a good lawyer?

I heard this from afar, but pretended not to. I knew my father only meant it as a thinly veiled boast, but it was a patronizing question, and one that our visitor was ill-equipped to answer. He had no knowledge of me, as we'd never exchanged more than small talk before.

The visitor was nice enough not to look in my direction. Instead, he said: I think Saeed would make a great lawyer. He has all the tools. And we need more of us in these powerful places.

I remembered that kindness, and that last line especially, almost fifteen years later, while sitting in the parking lot, a tangle of shock and shame. That visitor from long ago, whom I will call Ramzy, was now the chairman of the law firm that cancelled me. I had joined the firm in the first place because of him. Even though my law school marks qualified me to work anywhere, I picked his firm. We never became close friends, but I believed our family connection meant we'd be professional allies.

During my years working with him, I saw many examples of the near-total hold that Ramzy had on his firm. It seemed to me that he did not hesitate to exert his power in whatever way he deemed right. In my first summer there I remember being shepherded at his behest, along with dozens of other students and junior lawyers, to the Albany Club in downtown Toronto to fill space at an event for a new candidate of the Conservative party. This was not a political party I cared for, and the roundup distressed some who'd been subjected to it, but I thought: if nothing else, Ramzy has the courage of his convictions. He displayed it in other ways. A practicing Muslim, he frequently asked me during the firm's ultra-competitive student recruitment campaigns whether there were any superlative Muslim candidates to focus on. And few at the firm were ever left unaware of the dizzying array of charitable causes Ramzy backed.

So I thought of Ramzy in that parking lot because I thought he would see how misguided the cancellation was, what a travesty. I knew I was too proud to accept even a sincere offer to reverse the decision, but I wanted someone to at least tell me it had been a hasty, thoughtless mistake.

I sent him an email composed only of the subject line: "Interesting call I received from your firm just now."

The next day, he wrote asking when he could call.

My canceling happened during a relative lull in Israeli-Palestinian tensions. That made it somewhat atypical. In tranquil times, people are content to listen politely to contentious viewpoints, pursing their lips and shaking their heads at the appropriate moments of pathos, while remaining only a shade or two above indifferent. Injustice can have the air of the theoretical, a set of conditions that if feasible should be improved, but lacking the urgency of matters of life and death.

In flashpoints like an active, well-documented genocide, canceling or deplatforming takes on an existential importance. The reason is not the speaker, but their audience. In such times, the audience wants someone to narrate the goings-on with expertise or courage or eloquence, preferably all of them. In the case of the Palestinian genocide this desire was intense. It's not that people aren't capable of perceiving things well enough on their own, but that they ache to confirm they are not mad, that the revolt inside them is mirrored by revolt inside others. The desire for things to be articulated with honesty is the ultimate target of cancellation. Canceling an artist or intellectual is a handy shortcut to denying the desires of their audience, and in turn denying the audience the validation and empowerment to act.

The spaces that institutions provide are privileged spaces. Admittance is limited, and the constituency is for the most part highly educated, moneyed, and powerful. As the months of the genocide went by, institutions became far more careful about offering platforms to artists that may prove themselves disruptive. A typical institutional creature can tolerate a gaggle with a bullhorn in the street, so long as the privileged spaces where they spend most of their time are soundproofed from that racket. Seeing the increased withholding of available platforms, artists took it upon themselves to wrest the platforms away. That's when the spaces clarified themselves as exclusivist spaces, guarded by security guards, yes, but even before that guarded by the language of safety. We saw artist-led disruptions everywhere from prize galas, to book readings, to launch events throughout the Western world. In every instance, safety was used as pretext for the forcible removal of the protestors, and in some cases (as with the 2023 Giller Prize protestors) pursuing them with shaky criminal charges. The artists had become in their bodies the critiques they made in their art. By doing so, they were now threatening outsiders to the institutions they once belonged to or which once welcomed them.

It was not surprising that many, if not most, of these artists were of colour. Such artists know the falsity that is the polite indulgence of their work in the name of multiculturalism. They have long internalized that nothing real is achievable in such spaces without a severe sort of disruption, and they have existed in the margins for so long that being tossed back into them is not such a harrowing outcome.

What I found particularly compelling in these actions is the rather plain transformation of the artist into an activist. Their role as a witness of the world—as a witness of the bodies, the destruction, the erasure—led them into something more proactive, more urgent, less effete. The artists who protested the genocide were no longer content to challenge audiences with their *work*, they were challenging audiences with *themselves*, their objections to what was witnessed. Compelling people's attention is a fundamentally different endeavour from offering art as an optional experience. The work of the activist is bumptious, and requires the infiltration of spaces where they are unwanted. Mandating exposure to the expression of the artist creates a class of artist-activists.

The Palestinian genocide clarified certain artists as being at the vanguard of liberatory work. bell hooks has said that the self-expression that is at the usual core of art is a work of the liberation of the self. The work for the liberation of the self is personal, while the work for the liberation of a people is collective, but to me they feel connected. They are both about feeling free enough to express what needs to be expressed. Even if the mechanical steps of activism may seem foreign, the mental work required for it is familiar. The artist may not be a born activist, but it is a short hop to be made one.

Between when I was informed that my talk was canceled and when I spoke to Ramzy, about twenty-four hours passed. In that time, information had seeped out to me about what happened behind the scenes at the firm.

The book that I wrote was devoid of enough red meat to warrant cancellation, and indeed it seemed nobody had issues with the book itself. Instead, pricked by its title, two of the firm's partners had stalked my public Twitter account. Now, I have always been a judicious poster, the fingerprints of my father's caution all over my online conduct. Still, these partners evidently found posts objectionable enough to submit to the firm's leadership as evidence that I was unfit to be a guest of the firm. What posts these were, and why they were objectionable, I don't know. But the leadership accepted that my presence could endanger the "psychological safety" of the firm's employees.

Accounts varied on who comprised the leadership

group that made this decision. Some said the call was made by the firm's managing partner, a person who reported to Ramzy. Some said it was a group effort that included one of the firm's diversity leaders, a Jewish man with whom I'd become gym friends. Some said the decision had been made by the firm's highest authority, Ramzy himself.

I didn't know what to believe. But now that I'd had time to intellectualize some of the shame away, I wanted answers. I looked forward to speaking with Ramzy.

As I think of that phone call now, it is telling that I decided to take handwritten notes of it. Doing so was a deliberate act: in the minutes before Ramzy called, I fetched a pad and a pen, and placed them in front of me, next to my phone. I knew I'd want to write down what he said. Maybe I had hoped he'd have some affirming words I could use to erase the feelings that came with cancellation. But I also think it's likely I would not have felt the need to document a conversation with someone I thought of as a true ally, as opposed to as a representative of an institution that discarded me.

The call was anticlimactic. I did not get any answers. Instead, it was mostly Ramzy who interrogated me. I was shocked that I was having to answer any questions at all, but he wanted to know who delivered the news of the cancellation, how they delivered it, their exact wording, and what I'd been told about who made the decision.

When I pressed him on that last matter, he denied

being the decision-maker. He said that he was *aware* of the decision that was made, but that his input was not requested. So he did not stand in its way.

I turned this concept over in my head. The overall boss of the firm was briefed on an important decision, but his input wasn't specifically requested, so he did not stand in its way. It was frankly stunning.

I remembered what he, a visitor at my father's house all those years ago, had said. *We need more of us in these powerful places.*

As the call went on, Ramzy invoked our long-running familiarity and trust. He said: One day, a long time from now, we will sit down together, you and I, and I will tell you about all the shit that went down with this event. There's a lot that happened behind the scenes that you don't know about.

There was never any defensiveness, any sense of regret. It was like he wanted me to think we were both victims of the same circumstances. Except one of us was stripped of a platform, humiliated, and transformed into a figure of controversy and danger—and the other? The other was the head of the institution that did it.

Ramzy also told me that I should do what I have to do. He said this three times, at least, during the course of the conversation. I kept track of the number of times by way of vertical lines in my notes: "'You do what you have to do'—| | |"

Maybe he thought I might want to sue his firm. It explained his caginess about dispensing any more facts or rationale for the decision. Or maybe he was concerned that I would publish the story on my suddenly objectionable Twitter account, to generate online outrage and sympathy. (I was a new author, delighted to have even been published. Neither of those things were anywhere near my mind.)

The episode reminds me now of my grandfather Said languishing in Rafah, on the Egyptian border. The circumstances were vastly different, but for each of us, the fact of our Palestinianness had poisoned how our environment thought of us. Without that identity, I was an acceptable part of that firm. But with the identity, I was not acceptable, not at all.

We need more of us in these powerful places.

But what if we reached those powerful places? What would we do then?

For some, the answer is: nothing.

To an extent, I understood Ramzy's position. True, he'd accumulated, through his hard work and talent, an overwhelming amount of social and professional credit. True, he could've spent a pinch of that credit on reversing his firm's decision, or at least acknowledging its error in a private call with an old family friend. But maybe this is not what he wanted to spend his credit on. Maybe this was too explosive an issue for such an exercise of power. Maybe he understood that the price of belonging to institutions is wholesale conformance to their values. Maybe, as the head of the institution, he wanted to focus on positive, affirming things, things like "building bridges," or "thought leadership," or "DEI." I can only assume that my body as a Palestinian was adverse to all that.

(He wouldn't have been the only one to reach that conclusion. I was canceled again, a year later, during the genocide.)

I am told that the firm experienced a furor in the wake of my cancellation, with lawyers loudly objecting to it, and several complaints. A contentious all-hands meeting had to be held to placate those who were outraged. In the end, I have no doubt the institution felt it did the right thing in protecting the "psychological safety" of some of its members.

I also have no doubt this sort of safety paid dividends a year later, when the Gaza war started. That's when lawyers all over my country of Canada felt safe enough to sit in their office swivel chairs surveilling the social media accounts of other lawyers, especially juniors, in their firms, in case anyone posted or liked any posts sympathetic to Palestinians. Then they felt safe enough to type the names of such lawyers into Excel sheet blacklists, because they believed such social media activity was tantamount to support of terrorism. Then they felt safe enough to distribute these blacklists among themselves and between firms, as handy cheat sheets to consult carefully before considering anyone for employment.

Safety first, everyone.

– 6 –

The Company and You

Take this hypothetical.

Let's say the real estate market was in bad shape. Let's say they'd been spiking interest rates for a while now, trying to depress the soaring prices. It made sense in the macro, but was unhelpful to *you*, personally, at that moment.

You downloaded an app that tells you prices of houses recently sold in your area. A while back, you took a mortgage at what turned out to be the very peak of the market. But maybe the specific neighbourhood you picked was somehow immune to market forces? The app quickly informed you the neighbourhood was immune to nothing.

But what if *your* house was special. You had installed new pot lights in the family room. Every week you mowed your lawn with distinction and verve. You even weeded.

This must be what it feels like to spiral.

You pulled up your savings account. You've often thought banking should come with a trigger warning. You don't know what you expected to see.

You have art that could be sold. Collecting art for yourself is moral decadence anyway. There's that ugly 1970s lithograph you got for ten dollars from a curio shop in Puerto Rico, which turned out to be worth a few hundred when you looked it up. Or that sketch of an elephant you suspect is by a pretty good artist.

What can you return? The TV? The dining table? You heard you can return anything to Costco—what did you have from Costco?

It's important to determine how long you could rent a place, if need be. You counted up all your existing money (because you couldn't assume any future money). You pulled up a calendar on your computer and apportioned an equal amount to each of the little boxes that represented months, like you were sliding quarters and dimes across the table.

Your wife is tough, you don't need to worry about her feeling deprived. Your son can get loans for his university, it's not the end of the world. But you can't pull your three-year-old out of her swimming classes—she's too young and that's too cruel, no way.

But could she maybe live without a sprinkle donut *every* Saturday morning? It's a three-dollar donut. It adds up.

You can tell her it's a health decision.

You clicked back on the other window. The draft of your op-ed article was in the same state as before: done. It's been done for a while. You could have hit Send at that moment—or two hours before, or last night.

Instead, you tried finding ways to spend a few more minutes before you went ahead and exploded your whole life.

Few are the writers who write full-time. Most have day jobs to pay the bills. You are in the latter category. Your specific job, in case it matters, is lawyer at some company.

Let's say that joining your company was the culmination of a dream. You remember monitoring this company from afar for years before that. There was an obviousness to how much better it was than other companies in the industry, its work a model among its peers. But you were also attracted to the company's mission. *We just want to do good things for the world.* That's how the founders put it, right from the start. The thought that morality—a simple kind of morality, expressed without qualification—could be at the heart of corporate enterprise was alien and enchanting. The profits seemed to come effortlessly, almost an afterthought to the company's ethos.

Your first day at the company, you received a holographic employment badge that you attached to your waist. You kept it on even as you walked home after work, a secret pleasure to have it dangling at your side for strangers to see.

But now that you'd been there for some time, that old ethos didn't feel so critical anymore. The eternal thirst of shareholders meant the company had to keep pushing against the moral pillar supposedly at its centre, nudging it out of the way to allow revenues to flow with greater ease. You saw this happen in increments—a suspect contract gone ahead with here, a principle of conduct watered down there. But you still thought—at core, this is a *good* place.

You've always been aware of the tender spots of your association with your job. These are the areas that, if pressured too hard, could rupture like a boil, endangering how you think about your workplace, or your existence in it at all. The pessimist in you always thought a rupture of that kind was an inevitability; it was probably a trauma response from feelings like this in other parts of life. You've had years when your family was poor, and years when you were a young adult with a low income. Back then life was a state of getting by, head ducked, while knowing that something (a thin envelope, or a stern call) was en route to ruin it all by requiring you to deal with it.

You tried to convince yourself that your tender spots are run-of-the-mill, unremarkable. Insofar as enterprises of scale have economic relations with bad actors all the time, your company was hardly unique. Plus, you did not actually know the extent of your company's entanglement. There were conflicting reports about whether your company did or did not have a major contract with a genocidal state. The company itself says there is a contract, yes, but it's for a benign sort of services, very vanilla services, and not at all for military purposes. But there are many rumours in the public sphere otherwise. You don't know what to believe. Maybe your company's advanced capabilities help this particular state with tax audits, or maybe they help them identify the targets they are about to kill.

Knowing the truth is *far* above your pay grade. Your title makes you sound like some kind of powerful person at your company, but really you are just a functionary with limited information and responsibilities. You make no strategic decisions of any kind. Between you and the chief executive there are several layers of authority.

In the day to day, your tender spots with your job feel calm enough that you could disregard them. But in flashpoints—and there are always flashpoints—they pulse with heat. They become impossible to go on ignoring.

In those cases, your self-image changes overnight. You no longer see the version of yourself you spent years honing and repairing—an honourable person, a *good* person, and a capable professional at a company that brings you pride. Now you are transfigured in your mind into an unprincipled sell-out who is not ashamed to contribute to intense suffering.

You have to speak up, you think. You have no choice.

The crying does not distinguish between work and personal time. It has become a daily accident, liable to take place anywhere, anytime. When you feel it coming, you scramble to the washroom. If you see feet in an adjoining stall, you try to cry without noise. You didn't know this was possible, but you found that if you close your mouth and hold your nose at the same time, it can work. Breathing is difficult like that, yes, but the last thing you need is questions.

Your rule is to allow yourself three minutes for the crying. At one point there had been signs posted that suggested everyone take regular "micro-breaks"—twenty to thirty seconds worth of looking away from the monitor—as a way to refresh and replenish. And there you are basking in six times as much as the recommendation. Before you headed out of the bathroom, you checked that your cheeks were dry, and that you could reasonably claim your red eyes were only sleep-deprived.

You noticed that you walk much slower at work now, at a languorous, almost indulgent pace. Your professional posture has always focused on efficiency, so this is an odd development. Trips to the bathroom or the break-room now take you double what they used to. If a group of you walked to a meeting together, you were always the tail, forcing someone to awkwardly hold the door a little too long before you caught up. You tried to think of why your pace has changed. It dawned on you that when you're walking there is no possibility that you will look at a screen. The risk of exposing yourself to fresh trauma was reduced. Acting on its own, your body had installed a protective mechanism.

The meeting with your manager was short. He was understanding. He is an understanding person. He thanked you for giving him a heads-up, and said he looked forward to reading your piece when it comes out. When you told him you didn't think there was anything *really bad* in it, that it was just an appeal for humanity, he moaned with feeling. The critical thing was that he seemed to recognize it was not your intention to cause a ruckus specifically *at work*, although you realized it might happen. What you were doing was putting something out *there*, in the public sphere. (You motioned with your hands to show how far away you considered that sphere to be.) It was still less than ten days after the great catastrophic attack, the one everyone was encouraged to consider the new 9/11. You told your manager that if you didn't stick your neck out like this for your people, no one in this country would right now. As a writer you had the ability and the platform, so you felt you had to do it.

I'm sorry you felt you had to do it, he said, echoing the words you provided him. It sounded like sympathy for your feeling obliged to write, not regret that you did. But you never know. You always conjecture what guidance a middle manager may have been issued in times like this— whether what he said is what he's instructed to say, what he's allowed to say, or what he really wanted to say.

It was the end of the workday. On the train ride home, you pulled up the same list of available jobs on LinkedIn. What you considered most was not which jobs suited you. It was whether you should start applying now, before the stain of the article attached itself to you, or wait to apply after you'd been fired, so that you could find a workplace that didn't mind the stain.

That night, an online evening version of your article came out, much earlier than you'd expected. Within half an hour a senior salesperson messaged on the internal chat to congratulate you. It was very brave of you to write that, she said, blah blah blah. Your stomach turned. *Already* someone from work had seen it. Someone you were neither close to, nor trusted. *Already* things were out of control. You wondered how long it would be before everyone else caught wind. You were publishing in the biggest newspaper in the country—what did you think would happen?

You didn't bother going back to your job search. You had no doubt your name was already on the blacklist that had been circulated among legal departments and private firms in your country.

You discovered that genocides put you in the mood for deals.

The first deals you tried to make were directly with the people raining down all the missiles. You tried to convince them to target you instead of the kids who seemed to be their usual targets. You didn't make your offer via a formal letter or email or anything—you just sent it through normal telepathy, and sometimes (when you were really desperate) through prayer. But the deal was never really feasible. The children on that land over there were much more valuable than you on this land over here. Economically, it would've been a bad deal for the missile people.

There were other, more realistic deals. For example, when you saw the countless bodies dropping, you felt the need to make deals with them, the bodies. At the time, your conscience had such leverage on you that you felt you had no choice. But you hoped the countless bodies understood that you can only go so far. You live in the real world, and so they have to manage their expectations. This was the deal you came up with: You would speak up on behalf of the countless bodies in the public sphere, the sphere you told your manager about, but you could not speak up for them *at* work, or *in relation to* work. You would write articles and post to social media decrying the devastation and condemning the devastator, but you would not join any of the workplace actions, or use any of the various forbidden words at work. This plan would certainly jeopardize your livelihood, but only so much.

The countless bodies did not reply when you offered this deal. You took their silence as assent.

You decided on this because you understood that work is genocide-agnostic. Work always persists; this is not a defect, but a feature. Your direct deposit arrives like clockwork, notwithstanding any starvation or murder. In fact, you suspect that genocides may actually improve business. Genocide drives more consumption—of fuel, of machinery, of weapons, of raw materials, of technology—and business is founded on consumption.

The deal you gave the countless bodies was born out of years of analysis that you personally conducted, an unscientific but unending study that you call "How Brave Can I Be?" You had scrutinized the cases of those who lost their jobs due to their activism. Sometimes, a complaint came from outside the organization and threatened its reputation, so ties with the offending employee had to be severed. But often it was some internal conflict that originated the problems. Making your workplace a crucible for activism creates a distraction that threatens the profit momentum of the company. So it seemed reasonable that you eliminate that obvious source of risk.

You knew that your solution was hypocrisy of the plainest kind. But you found ways to justify it. You explained to yourself—very slowly, so you'd understand—that your actions do not affect only you, but your family, their residence, their food, their day-to-day lives. Think of all the layoffs going on, affecting people very like you, who used to sit at desks near you. Plus, you personally have done nothing wrong. You just move some papers, here and there, always for legitimate ends. Your hands are clean. Do you remember the six-hundred-some-page list of known Palestinian casualties, where the first fourteen pages were all infants? Well, if there were a similar detailed list of culpable people, the first *four hundred* pages might not include your name.

Finally, you reminded yourself that it makes no sense to add your body to the list of victims of this genocide. Your body is not bloody, gray, and dead, like the ones in all the telling pictures. But if you get yourself fired, is it not the body of a victim nonetheless? Your people need to be stronger, not weaker. No sense tossing your currently powerful—yet currently also powerless—body into the stove of a war that had already consumed so many.

Your wife has been helpful on this point. You are doing

so much already, she says, as she encourages you to decline another interview request. There are many who are silent, and you have not been silent. Get it out of your head!

Needless to say, the landscape of your friendships has changed. Some good friends you discarded as soon as they made a point of unfurling a blue-and-white flag on their social media, others tossed *you* away with similar speed. None of this perturbed you much, because you are used to sustaining this kind of damage. The main memories you have of close friends are of their being wrested away, so discarding people feels almost comforting to you now. You are not proud of this fact, but you can't dispute its truth.

Coworkers are a more delicate matter. As they are part of the transaction of employment, you are obliged to be careful with them. You could not get rid of them, so you took precautions. You looked up every name around you. If their affiliations could be ascertained indirectly somehow, you ascertained them. Did this one attend the synagogue that already started auctioning off parcels of land still piled with countless bodies? What about that other one—did you glimpse her in photos of the riots near you? Whatever it was, you tried your best not to evince a difference in how you treated them. When you sensed you were about to fail in your attempt to act normal, you tried desperately to mask it. It's not that I don't want to engage in convivial small talk with you, it's just that I have to look at my phone because of some urgent thing, you said, running.

Here and there a select few coworkers messaged you. Do you have a minute to talk? they'd ask. *In person*, they'd clarify. Text is ephemeral, but not ephemeral enough for topics like this. People will commit their marital affairs and racial prejudices to writing, but will not betray partiality to fewer dead Palestinian bodies.

In any event, soon you were having coffee with one of these coworkers. You discussed the recent rainfall, checked how old your respective children were this month. It must be so awful for you right now, they managed finally, the uncertainty of how to proceed almost overwhelming them.

What do you mean? you asked. You knew what they meant, but you acted stupid. You did not forget how assiduous they'd been in avoiding any engagement with your social media posts on the topic. It was a bravura performance of restraint, honestly. You were prepared to be cordial to them, but you would not permit them to offer you sympathy.

Just everything, they replied. The vagueness is on purpose. Describing what is awful must be too much of a commitment to its awfulness. Maybe they were afraid that you would quote them somehow. Whatever it was, they hoped you would let them off the hook and acknowledge their acknowledgement.

But you did not want to do that. Everything what? you said. Do you mean the flu bug going around?

No, I mean with what's going on in the world! It's so awful.

You reminded yourself that this was one of the good people. They were asking about you. Most hadn't bothered. Most have carried on as if the world still spun on the same axis it always has. But this coworker before you was different. They cared about you as a person, as a friend. And who knows what might happen if you continued to refuse them. Could they turn on you? You were already so alone.

Yes, it is awful! you answered. With such a mild February, we really are seeing climate change in real time these days, aren't we?

You looked them in their frustrated eyes. You thought: Tell me *what* is so awful, you coward.

You and a few other Palestinians from the company found each other. You were strangers before, from unrelated departments, but genocides cause people to scurry and clump. For safety, you decided to meet somewhere outside the office. At the office there were too many eyes, too many ears, too many complaint forms ready to be populated and submitted. So someone said let's meet at such-and-such café, where you can shake hands, commiserate, and strategize. A great idea, but you suggested a different place because, as you reminded your new friends, the original choice was subject to boycott.

The drinks you got were terrible. There was no freshness, none of the standards you're used to. But at least the table launched into the urgent matters right away. First, you reassured each other that, despite your advancing years, your memory did not lie to you about how the company reacted, less than two years prior, after Russia's invasion and plunder. The company had shed all its Russian business like it was picking a thread from its cuff, then asked all employees to lean into the task of aiding the hapless Ukrainians. Alright, good, you all said, satisfied that middle age has not yet bested you.

Then someone—a natural joker—asked if any of you planned to attend the "listening sessions" the DEI office had offered, intending them to be "safe spaces" to assuage the "challenging feelings of pain and upset" that some of our coworkers "of all backgrounds" may have been experiencing due to "the ongoing events." Oh yes, another replied, and while we're at it, why don't we just submit our wrists directly to the federal agencies and be done with it? The jokes piled on after that. It's good to feel light again, you all agreed.

Eventually came the serious question. One of the

others formed his hands into the shape of a box then pounded that box on the rickety table with each word he uttered: *I. Want. To. Know. What. We. Are. Allowed. To. Say!* You understood his frustration. He was an immigrant who had expected *this* country to allow him his convictions, or perhaps he was a naif who took the company's self-proclaimed goodness as an article of faith. In any event, the question was clearly addressed to you as the lawyer of the bunch. As a professional matter you cannot—and would *never*—give advice to these bedraggled, confused people. They are not your clients, the company is. You may be anguished, but not too anguished to remember your obligations. So you got philosophical. You said, Look, *hypothetically*, in a *hypothetical* workplace, there are always many words you cannot say, at the current time or any time. In any workplace there are more primordial values than genocide or ethnic cleansing or what have you. There is mission, revenues, professionalism. These aren't even pejorative values—we are all capitalists sitting around here, aren't we?—but they are *the* values. And no, fulfilling your work obligations is not enough to let you say what you want. There is a misconception that we are paid for doing work, when really we are paid for compliance. Our work is the main segment of our required compliance, but it is not the only part. (Here you felt you were expanding their brains in real time, like you were their guru.) Think of the professional activities that feel most like a waste of time. Our weekly syncs with managers. Our periodic touch-points with various teams, most of them overlapping in makeup and utility. Our workplace training sessions, on innumerable topics, requiring a certificate of completion, and refreshed each year, lest we forget. The sheets on the bulletin board telling us how long our micro breaks should be. Each of these are packets of information designed to instill a collective uniformity, an expectation that you evince in your workplace no innovation of thought or practice other than as explicitly solicited for your work. We cannot say the dotted lines weren't clear when half our work time is spent re-dotting them. Why then, do you think you should be allowed to *say something*, in this hypothetical company? Why do you think 'the ongoing events' are an exception?

Your colleague seemed confused. He asked you: Was it not you who started writing things in public months ago? And yet you still have your job. He looked worried that he'd confused you for someone else.

You nodded with a smug smile, a magician whose sleight of hand has baffled his audience. Since you like to be helpful, you decided to tell them your secret. You explained to your colleagues the deal you made with the countless bodies. You specifically pointed out that you have not signed any of the workplace petitions with sentences like *If the company does not cancel this contract, it risks being . . .* and demanding your company cleanse itself. You did not register with your superiors, for prompt escalation, your hurt feelings about the lack of action from your company. You did not respond to any of the emails from well-meaning workplace organizers who asked for testimonials of your lived experiences as a Palestinian, in an attempt to tug the heartstrings of management. You certainly did not line up with signs outside any of your company's office buildings and jabber to the press about all the ways your company has failed. You *most certainly* did not, and would never, join in occupying a high-ranking executive's office—the sort of executive who might know the content of any secret deals—to demand the company disclose and rescind these deals. Yes, you've spoken up, but you've kept work out of it.

But that's just you, you reminded the group. If you want courage, don't talk to a lawyer. They all chuckled, against themselves. You have always been good with the bon mots.

Must we be so scared? one of them looked about to say, but didn't. He must have seen the wisdom of your approach.

As a group, you resolved nothing, formulated no plan, and advanced no objectives—but on a personal level you left the meeting invigorated by your shared uselessness. They call this *community*, you reflected. As you said your goodbyes at the door, you all agreed to more meetings of this type, on a weekly cadence. Someone even sent a calendar invite. Professional to the very end, all of you, even in your personal hours. Everyone got in their cars and drove off. They were nice cars—recent models, and washed.

Despite the calendar invites, none of you made it to any more meetings like this.

You felt sick, in the clinical way. You had certain symptoms, none of which were important, even to you. In fact, you hurried to write the symptoms down when they occurred to you, so you'd remember what to say in case anyone asked why you're taking the day off.

Sickness reminds you of how meagre you are as a human. The weakness in being sick confirms how delusional is our customary conviction in our worth. When you took a sick day, the harsh fact is that someone else subbed for you. This someone was not as brilliant as you, did not quite have your acumen or experience—but they reviewed what needed to be reviewed, and commented where comment was requested, just like you would have. This is because your expertise, however specialized, is limited. Enterprise of any scale is composed of dozens of replaceable bit players, assembly line workers notwithstanding their high degrees and higher airs. This fact does not bruise your ego—it is what lets you take two-week vacations and knock off from work early on Fridays so you can fire up the barbecue. That you're not required for the system gives you a measure of distance. And distance breeds unaccountability. No one on the assembly line is responsible for the whole of the line. You do not have the skills to complete the entire project on your own, nor did anyone consider asking you to do it. It's a delicious freedom! Are there any sweeter words than "It's not my job"? Now, it does also mean that your views about the whole are irrelevant. Actually, almost everyone's views are irrelevant, with the exception of a few select souls who are in ultimate charge.

That means there is very nearly *no one* accountable for the whole. The whole exists on its own, beyond the reach of our petty disagreements with it.

This is why you have an implicit understanding that the supposed secret contracts are not yours to comment on or even inquire about. They are beyond your role. And in the irresistible logic of the company, going beyond your role is a contravention.

But, as it happens, you were in the mood for contravention. As your protest against this oppressive system, and despite having taken a sick day, you logged into your work machine to answer a few emails. Your fill-in wasn't getting to them quickly enough.

— — —

THE COMPANY AND YOU

One C-suite executive in your company seemed to recognize the trauma impacting his employees. You don't
remember exactly what the executive said, to be fair. It
was at one of those massive all-hands during which you
sank into some purgatory between attention and inatten-
tion, reality and hallucination. At a certain juncture the
question of the countless bodies bubbled up somehow—a
minor miracle. And what you think you heard from the
executive is that, in trying times, certain employees might
find that their personal values no longer align with those
of the company—at least, not as well as they used to. Such
introspection, and any recalibration it elicits, is healthy,
even necessary. If the result is that some employees decide
to part ways with the company, the company would certainly wish them well. The company would even admire
them for their principles.

Now that you write it down, it sounds very much
like a hallucination. A senior executive would not make
such statements or invitations—they simply would never.
The truth is your recollection cannot be trusted, as you
had been sedating yourself at the time. You are not one
for pharmaceuticals, but you did not even need them.
The algorithms had been adjusted by then. Instead of
the countless bodies, your social media now comprised
a revitalizing melange of home improvement hacks, co-
medians skewering their audience members, and the life
philosophies of Kobe Bryant. You applied this soothing

protocol to yourself like a moisturizer, before work, after work, and before bed. Soon you noticed that your dramatics had diminished. The unseemly crying went away. One of your coworkers even complimented you on your sunny disposition of late—That's the you we like to see, pal! The narcotized you was the better-adjusted you, the more reasonable you, the you that walks faster to meetings and mishears executives, the you brimming with life and mission.

Not everyone found a protocol like yours. One woman (a Moroccan, or a Lebanese, or a Pakistani, or a Black, or a Native, or a Jew, or someone like that, you can't quite remember) sent an email to everyone in the company—hundreds of thousands of people—announcing her moral decision to quit her job. *I cannot in good conscience put my own interests above all the murdered children*, she wrote, *and this company's continuing* . . . but you skipped the rest of the email, which went on for several more paragraphs in what you presumed was the same vein.

You admired her, and she also repulsed you. Even sedated, you could not deny that you felt deep inside you the yen to wash yourself in the waters of abandonment. But what an ego on that person to actually do it, to actually quit.

It really is just ego. It is ego that deludes you into thinking that you, the minor character that you are, can make a difference. It is ego that makes you think that because you have a reputable profession you are important, that makes you think you could organize your life in a freer, more honest way than others, than your father even, ego that makes you think your *voice*—that vacuous, self-important word—is worth anything, can change any minds, or is even worth listening to in the first place. If you can loosen the death grip your ego has on you, you would see with greater clarity. Your selfish desire to placate the buzzing gnat that you call your conscience is a disrespect to all the years your ancestors spent trying to get you to this position of privilege. (Yes, specifically *you*, the child they once swung by the arms between them, comforting themselves for a moment with the thought that they could shield you from the want and anguish they had to endure.) Your selfishness is a rejection of your responsibility to prosper. Your selfishness is imagining that you can have both a good job and undefiled scruples. Your selfishness is a surrender to the individualistic virus that infects this culture, the virus that drifts in your blood, whispering as it travels that you—and your personal feelings, your personal needs, your personal values—supersede all. Your selfishness is that you entertain leaving your (actual) dream job, which you perform alongside (actually) wonderful colleagues, on projects that are (actually) important. Your selfishness is that you think you are some latter-day prophet warning the world of calamitous depravities, when the world has already been warned by millions of other prophets brandishing their smartphones like fresh scripture. Your selfishness is reassuring yourself that your wife is tough, that your son can withstand some education debt, that your toddler should not have a *fucking donut*—just because you could not clench your teeth and bear a mental kind of pain, a pain that leaves as its mark, what, a wrinkle or two on your ugly forehead? A pain that has landed on many before you, and they took the lashing and went on anyway. Your selfishness is that you are willing to give away any part of your life—the life that belongs to generations before you, the generation alongside you, and generations after you—just to quit.

If you erased your ego—your self—you'd be able to exist much better.

The business about quitting made you think of someone, from long ago, someone who did not quit. Eventually, you found the right keywords to unearth her.

There were many articles, from presses all around the world. The articles mostly carried the same black-and-white photograph from 1943, when Irmgard Furchner was an eighteen-year-old woman embarking on her first day as a professional. Irmgard is smiling, her cheekbones like orbs. Her hand held possessively onto the latch of the door to the brick building of her office, near modern-day Gdańsk, Poland. Irmgard did not have a holographic employment badge like you did on your first day of work, but she was probably issued a key so she could let herself in and out. Irmgard probably treasured this key, even if it was the key to a concentration camp.

When you realized you'd one day be on trial, you devoured all the articles you could find about Irmgard, to make sure you had all the information. Her specific role at the camp was secretary to the Stutthof camp commandant. She read and wrote letters and telegrams and kept records. The role was clerical, menial. Her office was crowded with many desks for other bureaucratic staff like her. She had nearly no contact with the prisoners or the prison. The Stutthof camp had originally been set up with the goal of exploiting prisoners for forced labour, but over the course of Irmgard's two years of employment there, it was converted from a labour camp to an extermination camp. The figure the articles gave was 10,505. That's how many human beings—mostly Jews—the Nazis killed at Stutthof during Irmgard's two years there.

In this moment you pined for the sense of blasé detachment you had a few years ago when you learned about Irmgard then tossed her aside as a figment of remote history. You have lost that luxury for good. Now, you could not help pulling up the German trial court decision on her case. Irmgard was put on trial in 2021 when she was ninety-six years old. They plucked her out of the Hamburg retirement home where she lived and parked her wheelchair behind the defendant's table. Then the prosecution laid out the monstrous crimes that were committed in the camp. There was a parade of witnesses and historians testifying in minute detail, as if such things needed testimony or corroboration anymore. The German judges presiding over the case did not entertain any arguments that the people in the camps may have deserved what they got, that they were criminals, or animals or whatever. The withering words of the court were that the victims of the camps *could not be blamed for anything except that they had the wrong ancestry, religious affiliation, sexual orientation or political views*, and that this should have been *obvious even to an eighteen-year-old with Nazi upbringing.*

Irmgard was but a secretary, a stenographer for her boss. She did not commit the atrocities herself or direct the soldiers or executioners. Her lawyers said that a young woman like Irmgard would have been shielded even from knowing the purpose of her workplace by her superiors, men who used euphemism to disguise the crimes they were committing: "evacuations" when they meant death marches, and "special treatment" when they meant gassing. There was scant evidence to contradict this in the correspondence Irmgard had typed up for her boss.

The German judges were not satisfied. They slipped on their overcoats and took a field trip to the site of the former Stutthof camp. They stood in the spot where Irmgard's office had once been, eighty years ago, and surveyed the geographical landscape, which they supplemented with site plans and old photos of the prison. They imagined what Irmgard's sightlines would have been when she walked around in her office, which windows she could look through, whether she could see the gate to the concentration camp or the chimney of the crematorium, and whether there would have been any trees standing in her way. The judges were satisfied that, even from Irmgard's building, which did not closely adjoin the camps, she could not avoid witnessing the prisoners. She saw *their catastrophic physical condition, their lack of food and adequate clothing, and the deplorable hygiene conditions.* She heard their cries and smelled their burning.

It occurred to you that at least you could not smell anything from your smartphone.

Irmgard's lawyers argued that she had no power to change anything in the camp, because she was only a functionary. The judges accepted this argument. They couldn't even find that Irmgard had any desire to kill the prisoners.

Still, it was enough for them that Irmgard was *available to camp management as a reliable and obedient subordinate*, that she was *part of a system of subordinates who did not question the orders*. By just doing her job, the judges felt that Irmgard provided *psychological support* to the camp management and the rest of the camp system while they committed their crimes.

For a fleeting moment you may have thought it was strange that these judges somehow did not seem to value the safeguarding of workplace psychologies. After that, what really struck you was that, if you took yourself far enough away from that figure of 10,505 killed, you could almost feel sorry for Irmgard for having lived in a time and place when her mere professional compliance as a teenaged employee resulted in a humiliating trial in her doddering nineties. But for the judges, a key to convicting Irmgard was that she could have quit but didn't.

The defendant could have ended their work at any time without relevant negative consequences.

You rifled through the court's decision for what might qualify as a "relevant negative consequence." The best you could tell, it meant that Irmgard was not enslaved. She was not physically forced to work. Irmgard could have drafted a letter of resignation and handed it to the camp commandant, and he would've done no worse than shake her hand and wish her well.

A *relevant negative consequence* for Irmgard did not

seem to include losing her income, defaulting on her mortgage, or selling her art collection.

Precedent is the basis of the law. So when you are tried, who knows how many years later, some relentless prosecutor, possibly not yet born, will point to all your similarities to Irmgard. The prosecutor will stand up in court and say it is no defence that you were a mere functionary. The prosecutor will say that, yes, Irmgard may have only had to look over her shoulder to see the death camps, but you only had to do something just as effortless: look at your phone. The prosecutor will peer at the jury with certitude in her eyes, and she will explain how both you and Irmgard gave your respective superiors the *psychological support* they needed to do their work. You made it easy for them to facilitate the countless bodies. (And of course the prosecutor will detail the atrocities that led to the countless bodies, for lawyerly completeness, not necessity—by then, the jury will have been convinced of them for decades.)

There will come a point when the prosecutor might decide to philosophize. The jury research her team conducted will have indicated that this jury would appreciate a deeper dive, something to accentuate the weightiness of the matter before them. The prosecutor will say Irmgard is actually *very* similar to the accused (she calls you the accused, always, as if she couldn't be bothered to learn your name, because there are so many of your ilk). Our society today is no longer run by governments like the one that ran the concentration camp. It is run, the prosecutor will say, by corporations whose insidious reach goes much further and deeper than any government. We have come to privilege corporatism over civic responsibility as a reflex, because our corporate selves are the selves we most identify with, those *whole selves* we were encouraged to bring over and idealize, the selves whose responsibilities are most clearly defined, whose new moralities are encoded in handbooks on which we have initialed our binding acceptance. But that is *not* how it should be, the prosecutor will shout, pounding with her fist the ledge of the jury box. We have to recognize how wrong this is! The social contract should never take a back seat to the employment contract. The least Irmgard should have done is quit her masters, and the same goes for the accused. The point is, whether they are governments or corporations, they are *not* our masters, they are only what we allow them to be.

True, your lawyers will have their turn too. They will jump up from their seats utterly indignant. This prosecutor has the gall to compare an ordinary company to a concentration camp? Is she out of her mind? Nothing this company did is different from what thousands of other companies did—they provided services and charged fees! Companies do that all the time, everywhere, with everyone! A company is now responsible for the vileness of its customers? What absolute drivel. This whole proceeding is an outrage.

The jury will be taken by this show of passion. And once your lawyers have calmed down, they will painstakingly point out all the differences between you and Irmgard. Let's not hurt our heads with philosophy like our dear prosecutor over there, okay? one of them will chuckle, trying to get a laugh out of the jury, to make things reasonable again. A concentration camp has a singular purpose, they will point out, and that is to imprison, torture, and kill. Meanwhile, your company provided services of a far more abstract, multifunctional nature. None of your direct superiors were real decision-makers, so whatever *psychological support* you provided to them didn't actually matter. Most crucially, your lawyers will argue that Irmgard knew what her camp did, while you were always under a blanket of uncertainty about what exactly your company did. How could you be liable for a crime you weren't even aware of?

In the hours while you await the verdict, stealing glances at your young grandchildren sitting confused in the back of the courtroom, your lawyers will pat you on the shoulder and say they are confident you will be fine. Okay, they will say, let's suppose you had a hunch about what was going on at your company—you can't be expected to take action based on a hunch. No one gets convicted because they had a hunch.

At least, let's hope the jury sees it that way, they will probably add.

Lawyers always hedge.

As you're waiting, you thought that maybe a prison sentence wouldn't be the worst thing after all. This was probably the sickness talking. When you've been half in love with easeful death for so long, any kind of penance might seem a relief.

But in the end you know a court's punishments don't actually matter. The real courtroom is in your mind. The proceedings there go on forever and the rules of evidence are irrelevant. Hunches are more than enough. There, you can't depend on the gray areas, or caution against oversimplification, or plead reasonable doubt.

In your mind you feel like you are covered with crusted pigeon droppings, made permanent by a scalding heat. The stains feel like they will never go away.

This entire lengthy hypothetical was disingenuous. You were going to ask yourself a question at the end of it, hoping for absolution to come from complexity. But is the question even necessary now? Was it ever?

There is one word that has become overused. It has been slapped around seemingly against everyone, all the time: against governments, companies, politicians, tax-payers, friends. But you have avoided saying it. You've not said it of others, because you are kind, and you've not said it of yourself, because you are a liar. That word comes back to you whether you want it or not, an insistent incantation that you can hear all the time, over every commotion.

There was never a question of whether you're complicit.

– 7 –

Imagination

As a general matter, I do not have a strong talent for looking at my past. This exercise in witnessing the Palestinian genocide side by side with my own life was not something I relished. But as the genocide had left me, like most, at a loss, I thought I needed the study. A study in the uncertain steps of the past to learn how to venture into the future.

I don't want it misconstrued as humility that I profess to have come up with no grand answers. The problem is bigger than me, and I do not have it in hand. What I have are some shards of desires, all originating in a feeling that will not be suppressed.

Let me start with the feeling. It came after a stout, septuagenarian uncle-type walked up to yell at me at the conclusion of one of my talks.

This was more than a year into the genocide. My rhetoric by then had gotten much less timorous. Whatever I said must have triggered something for him, because this Palestinian man strode over with purpose, brushing away others with whom I was conversing. Then he began jabbing a finger in my chest as he informed me, in Arabic, what our community lacks. We lack—and only for this he switched to English—*soft skills*. The soft skills we all have to use at work, he said. You know those?

He explained that the youth—like *me*, I think he meant—don't understand that we cannot be so confrontational at our protests, that we cannot cover our faces like common criminals, and be so crazy with our slogans. In a low tone, he confided: Me and you understand that Israel is the problem, but we can't go out in big trucks downtown and say it that way! We always have to hope things get better, but saying the wrong things only makes them worse. Only stretch your legs as far as the length of your mattress—you know that proverb, akhi?

What was notable to me about that man's attitude is how hard Israel itself had worked to foster in us something very much like it. The country persists on the back of an existential fear it has planted in the Jewish diaspora, a fear that positions the Palestinian as the ultimate antagonist of the Jew. From there was installed a powerful infrastructure for denying Palestinian life, an infrastructure that Israel keeps running at Medium during times of merely humdrum oppression, but always ready to turn up to unimaginable levels of burning, as needed.

Creating in Palestinians a fear for our bodies was the indispensable starting point, the linchpin for enforcing all the other depredations. The fear makes it so that leaving the homeland where we were born, where we lived and formed an identity, feels almost a relief, even if we end up sacrificing both our identities and our dreams in favour of clawing for modest immediate needs. Soon we discover the language allotted to us—in our occupied land and in estrangement—is different from the language available to others, such that we are disabled from putting into words what we want or what we imagine. Our stories are limited and mangled, if we are even permitted to tell them at all. The people who speak for us are suppressed, lest they voice our forgotten humanity. And assertion of our selves is forever constricted by economic systems designed to put making a livelihood above all else, including asserting ourselves as a people.

The combination of these various oppressions—and a thousand others like them—is what exiled my grandfather, silenced my father, and forced me into invisibility for much of my life. The oppression stifled what was possible. It made it seem, in our hearts most of all, that our best option was a frictionless integration and low expectations.

So I understood the pain of that man who yelled at me and jabbed my chest. He is like all of our family's generations rolled into one. My innards crumpled when I recognized that about him. I listened to him for as long as he said what he needed to say. I did not contradict him.

But the feeling I cannot suppress is that I will not accept leadership from his likes anymore. I refuse to substitute inert, cautious hope where there should be struggle. Enough is enough. There is a point at which we internalize too well the bitter lessons the tyrants have taught us, such that we cannot conceive of any true rebellion against them.

Once, my father told me that he wanted to write a book about his life.

I remember that I was looking at a computer screen. My father materialized in the doorway, his face glowing with inspiration. It was like he'd just had the most dazzling idea and wanted me to confirm its genius.

At times during our relationship, my father tried to be my friend. His main way in those moments was to divulge. He'd tell me something personal, in the hope that I might join in what he was feeling. Do you want me to show you the *best* shawarma place? he'd say, bursting with greedy conspiracy. Guess what prize I just got? he'd ask, hoping that his professional accolades could be a matter of my fervent speculation.

But I was hardened by our years of antagonism after our arrival in America, those years when I received (and instigated) the brunt of his frustrated temper. I didn't rebuff his attempts at friendship in flagrant ways. Instead,

I met him with distance, with curtness, with avoidance, and with deception. I'd go to the shawarma place, but at a later time, by myself, and I wouldn't give him the satisfaction of matching his happiness when I reported back. I'd inquire about that prize he'd been awarded, but with an air of disinterest that all but nullified the inquiry. Even when we were happiest, I had a barrier against my father that I was too cruel not to lower.

And in this moment of vulnerability that he shared with me, as he told me about his secret aspiration, I did not deviate from my usual course of conduct. I said, without looking up: That's an interesting idea.

My father was too pleased with himself to let it go like that. The book I'm envisioning would be about my journey, he said, which is a big journey of overcoming and success.

I replied: Do you think that's enough?

I measured out my words like drops of poison.

I don't remember exactly why I answered that way. Maybe I just wanted to stifle his excitement. Maybe I was worried he'd ask me to help him write his story. But I think I may have truly believed there was not enough there. I thought: my father may consider himself remarkable, but he is an immigrant like any other. As a Palestinian, he may have had extra obstacles to overcome, but there was no way to talk about them even if we wanted to. So what's left?

My father's eyes dropped. He murmured: Yes, well I'd put other things in there, too . . . Anyway, let's think about it. Yalla, okay, I'll leave you to your work.

My father died a few years later, having never written that book about his life. My response was probably not the reason. His life was always full—with family, work, travel, and infirmity.

Still, I not only declined to help him tell his story, I actively discouraged it. Even our survival felt of a quotidian category, a survival many others had managed as well as we had. We were not extraordinary.

My memory is quicksand. I forget what I don't write down on scraps of paper, or email to myself. I forget what I don't tell everyone about. I forget what I do not mythologize.

When I was nearing forty, the death of my father struck me for a second time. Not like a bad memory, but like it was happening anew. By then it had been eight years since he passed, and the pain had dissipated to manageable levels. And yet as I approached that square age—that age of maturity—his death rushed at me again, bewildering with freshness. I gathered my son and went to visit his grave. There was that tombstone, the gray rectangle flush on the ground, its Arabic scripted with my own imperfect calligraphy, disclosing the insufficient life summary that I had drafted.

IMAGINATION

الدكتور أحمد سعيد الطيب

DR. AHMAD SAID TEEBI

PHYSICIAN, SCIENTIST

POET, PALESTINIAN

My father had died young, at sixty-one. Cancer had ended his life, but not before it teased us with the possibility of staving it off. The doctors excised its locus of growth, which was his tongue. For his last year, my father was speechless. He could not say a word. The looks he gave us became meaning, because all he had left were looks.

As I stood by his tombstone, I understood why his death had come back to me again. Forty was my father's age when we were displaced to North America. It was a dividing line in how I thought of him. It was then that, for me, he transformed from (a) a person to (b) a person who had lost things. He had lost our family's entire life, his own entire life. All he worked for in his second life was to somehow regain a semblance of the first.

Everything on his tombstone that I wrote after his life ended at sixty-one, I could have also written had he died at forty.

In comparison, at my own forty, I felt meagre. What would my tombstone have said at that point? Having not been saddled with even half my father's troubles, I'd not been half the man he was. I thought fate would not be unjust if it granted me the same lifespan as my father. In fact, I thought it would be generous.

So I wrote the moment down, so I would not forget. I did a little arithmetic, and then I made a plan for my next twenty-one years.

It was a to-do list for self-improvement, a list of desires for myself, with actionable goals and deadlines, and every bit as clichéd as it sounds. I kept its contents secret, and I still do. But these dreams could no longer be quicksand to me, now that they were written.

What I wanted most out of that list were two things: to not fail my father's legacy, and for those writing my tombstone to not wonder too long what to write.

Hundreds of thousands of Palestinians perished in the genocide in the many months during which it went on, but I have some moments left before my tombstone is etched.

I remember the Fridays during the war when I went to a nearby mosque. I was famished most of all for the imam's voice in qunoot, praying within prayer. His trembling voice witnessed the martyred and mutilated, and asked for their salvation and their liberation. The collective wept with him in pain and asking. I wept too, most of all from awe at the frankness of the supplication. It was a frankness born of desperate, torn souls resorting to a higher power, making their desires as plain as they could. It was not honest, it was an honesty.

For myself—and for all those who count themselves like me—here is a tangle of my own desires, as shimmering with honesty as I can make them. In the future I wish that they may catch me with their glint, when I find myself in the murk of forgetfulness.

As a beginning, I want the pain to never leave me. I want to feel it in my heart always, like lead. I want to never bury it, never have to resort to whispering to my children's children in shame or in code. There is use in being haunted, if you can remember how you came by your ghosts.

I want what we witnessed to not bear as its fruit defeat, but obstinacy. I want to never forget the man who watched his home be leveled by a missile, only to return to the smokey and hot scene, unfurl a folding chair, and sit cross-legged on the rubble to smoke a cigarette, as if the destruction had barely inconvenienced his afternoon. I want us to embody that kind of jakara—part spite, part insouciance, all defiance.

I want to always know our worth—the extraordinary among us and the ordinary—despite all that would make us feel cheap and disposable.

I want to never let myself feel imprisoned, even if there are prisons readied for me everywhere, as small and decrepit as I am willing to accept. Our worst chains are often those we wear of our own accord.

I want to relive that feeling that chilled me, the one that came when I considered—with as much candid introspection as I could muster—whether I was capable of committing the kind of acts the Israelis committed. The feeling that haunted me was: If they were human, and I am human like them, couldn't I, too, by some sort of human transitive property, kill like them? If I transformed myself with enough ideology and rhetoric and righteous indignation, couldn't I put on a uniform and kill a child because of the curls on the sides of his head, or because his parents speak and do things odious to me and mine? I want to remember the chill that this thought brought me, the revulsion I felt for it in my sinews. No, I could never. I would never. No one human should ever. I want that rejection to come and come again.

I want to remember that my morality is encoded in everything I say or write. What I express is an indication of my preoccupations, and what I don't express also an indication. And the only morality I really care about is truth. Not lies, not partial truths, not the truth contorted into a figure that my enemy won't target me for, that my acquaintances can mildly espouse, that my publisher can live with, that my family or my friends or my clerics want from me, the truth that will sell books or attract followers, the truth that will keep me safe, the truth that will keep my children clothed and schooled and their bodies plump.

I want to never revert to lying.

I want to revel in being marginal, of existing in the liminal spaces, if that is my fate for telling the truth.

I want to be gentle with those who succumbed to the feeling of weakness in their hearts, who lunged for the safety of conforming—the ones who decided to do nothing. But I want them to know that my gentleness does not mean they haven't failed, because they have. I don't believe that every human is required to be consumed with every injustice in the world. But an extermination of any people, if countenanced and endorsed, is an extermination of human values. I want to remember every person for whom this is not a primordial concern.

I want to be certain, as Mahmoud Darwish was, that clarity is not a fault, and having a message and communicating it is not a barbarism. I want the knots in our tongues, the ones to which we have for so long been resigned, to be untied.

I want us to allow ourselves to refuse receipt of the doctrines of our states and our workplaces. It may feel lonely to do so, but only because it is the work of these systems to make you feel like a speck in their machinery, to make you feel lonely, even if you are not alone.

I want to internalize that a platform is useless if it is not deployed when most needed. I want to remember that power is not power if never discharged when most needed.

I want to make my truth-telling body—my presence

as a human being and as a writer—a danger to those who want to preserve their psychological safety, because safety for psychopathy is a danger to everyone. In itself, speaking out is an imaginative act, because it contains within it the conviction that a different future is possible.

I want to remember that, as Edward Said stated, it is the duty of intellectuals to find an alternative way, a way that isn't endorsed by a society that seeks to preserve the cruel status quo. I want to remember that, as Nizar Banat said, defeat has to be manufactured, and that it is intellectuals who have to accept defeat as logical and just, before it becomes palatable for everyone else. I want to never manufacture defeat.

I want to take on the challenge of writing a story that has not been written, that is forbidden to be written, a story that occurs in a history that has not been accepted. I want to remember that artists can make even the oldest problems urgent and terrifying, that our perspective of the world tilts by the hands of the artist. I want to believe that we can be the shift in perspective.

I want that, if the day comes that I am put on trial, I have things to say in my defence, a pittance though they may be. I want to say that I did all I could, even if I did not do everything I wanted.

I want to dream larger than ceasefires, larger than restoring, larger than making our prisons more comfortable.

I want to remember what Ghassan Kanafani said about

revolutionary literature being born in times of relative prosperity, and I want, as an exile, to recognize my relative prosperity, my relative safety. I want to create the mythologies that will innervate our future selves.

I want to go back, frequently, to that moment when, in the midst of the genocide, in the midst of the grayness of death, my cousin Abed in Germany sent me illustrations he'd created of a future Palestine. City after city shimmered with the gold hues of stone and sunshine. Olive trees, somehow both aged and modern, were the centrepieces of public squares. I remember especially the gnarled tree by the shore of his future Jaffa, boats bobbing in the blue water behind it. I want to dream like he dreams.

I want to keep in mind, always, how far we've come, even if it has often seemed we've been digging into concrete with a spoon. I want to dig through all the concrete still there, and the concrete that is forever being readied for our future.

I want us to be steeled in our newfound communities as they revealed themselves in these darkest of times, because it is through them that our resolve was consolidated, that we determined our plurality. The communities that were once forced to hide their meetings for fear of reprisal from police and terrorists, but now do not shy from taking any space to state their urgent case, even at ever-increasing costs.

I want for my mind to always reverberate with the sound of the freedom to come. I want to remember the man who threw open the doors of a dungeon prison in Damascus, revealing the women and children who had been locked in it for years. The doors were open wide in front of them, but they did not approach. They looked confused and anxious, having not comprehended that the regime had fallen overnight. They were immobilized with fear. I want my mind to forever be filled with the words of that man who told them, sonorous as a poem:

Don't be afraid,
Don't be afraid,
Don't be afraid,
Go, go,
Don't be afraid.

I want to remember that at so many times in my life, and especially when the genocide started, I thought I'd been struck speechless, that I could never write another word—and that I was wrong.

I want to find for myself the devil-may-care noisiness of my four-year-old daughter, the soul of my soul. I remember her riding trains with me and her mother, on our way to protests. But she didn't wait for us to get there to begin her calls. Right on the train, she'd climb on her seat and belt out *Free, Free Palestine* in her sweetly hoarse voice, as if none of the pursed lips and discomfited eyes around her mattered. I want for myself the cultural dissonance that she personified, because living despite the dissonance—as unaware of it as possible, or even panto-miming unawareness—is such great freedom.

I want to think, always, of the souls of our souls. Our children, and the children of others.

I want to never *hope*, to never be stuck in its expectant static. I want to always imagine, because there is nothing that compares with the engine of imagining.

And last is not something I want, but something I vow: They will not kill our imagination.

By now, it has become clear to me that this is one of those books in which the grand triumph of its narrator is the writing of the book itself. I wish I could've done something about this, but the reality is what it is. This book exists because I challenged myself to loosen the chains that once made anything like it feel impossible.

My father ran out of time to write his autobiography. It is tempting to think this book approximates what he would have written, or to think of it as my way of fulfilling my father's desire that I quashed all those years ago.

But that wouldn't be true at all. This book is far too divulging for my father's taste, too confrontational, too much of a danger to the people whose stories it tells. My father may have felt vindicated to read such a book, and it may have even inspired him—so long as he knew it was written by and about some distant family, not his own.

But if I exceeded the language and the stories that my father permitted himself, if I said things he'd have never said, it was because what I wanted to honour are not the practices he moulded out of fear, but the love that made him come up with those practices in the first place.

The only true way to honour the dead is to work for futures that would've saved them.

Acknowledgements

There is no scale of acknowledgement large enough to suffice those who have suffered, and continue to suffer, in Palestine. I can only ask for their forgiveness.

In writing this book, I relied on the works of many writers, but chiefly Edward Said, Ghassan Kanafani, Rosemary Sayigh, Rashid Khalidi, and Raja Shehadeh.

In instances where I quoted lines of Arabic poetry, I am to blame for their English translations.

Thank you to my agent Martha Webb for her ardent championing of this book. Thank you to my editors Nicole Winstanley and Brittany Lavery at Simon & Schuster Canada for taking it on, whole, and raising it up. Thank you to the University of Western Ontario for giving me time and space to write. Thank you to my siblings, my son, and my wife for their thoughtful commentary and tolerance of me. Thank you to my father, who was my greatest inspiration, and to my mother, who was my greatest source.

© Sarah Köhler

Saeed Teebi is an award-winning writer and lawyer. His debut short story collection, *Her First Palestinian*, was a finalist for several awards, including the Atwood Gibson Writers' Trust Fiction Prize. His nonfiction has appeared in *The Globe and Mail* and *The New Quarterly*. Born in Kuwait, he resettled in the United States, then Canada.